THE **COLOR** OF **COMPROMISE**

STUDY GUIDE

T0308495

THE **COLOR** OF **COMPROMISE**
STUDY GUIDE

JEMAR TISBY

with *Tyler Burns*

ZONDERVAN REFLECTIVE

ZONDERVAN REFLECTIVE

The Color of Compromise Study Guide
Copyright © 2020 by Jemar Tisby

Published in Grand Rapids, Michigan, by Zondervan. Zondervan is a registered trademark of The Zondervan Corporation, L.L.C., a wholly owned subsidiary of HarperCollins Christian Publishing, Inc.

Requests for information should be addressed to customercare@harpercollins.com.

Zondervan titles may be purchased in bulk for educational, business, fundraising, or sales promotional use. For information, please email SpecialMarkets@Zondervan.com.

ISBN 978-0-310-17433-2 (softcover)

ISBN 978-0-310-11484-0 (ebook)

Unless otherwise noted, Scripture quotations are taken from The Holy Bible, New International Version®, NIV®. Copyright © 1973, 1978, 1984, 2011 by Biblica, Inc.® Used by permission of Zondervan. All rights reserved worldwide. www.Zondervan.com. The "NIV" and "New International Version" are trademarks registered in the United States Patent and Trademark Office by Biblica, Inc.®

Any internet addresses (websites, blogs, etc.) and telephone numbers in this book are offered as a resource. They are not intended in any way to be or imply an endorsement by Zondervan, nor does Zondervan vouch for the content of these sites and numbers for the life of this book.

All rights reserved. No part of this publication may be reproduced, stored in a retrieval system, or transmitted in any form or by any means—electronic, mechanical, photocopy, recording, or any other—except for brief quotations in printed reviews, without the prior permission of the publisher.

Cover design: RAM Creative
Cover photo: Everett Collection Historical / Alamy Stock Photo
Interior Design: Kait Lamphere

Printed in the United States of America

24 25 26 27 28 29 30 31 32 33 34 35 /TRM/ 18 17 16 15 14 13 12 11 10 9 8 7 6 5 4 3 2 1

CONTENTS

Preface vii

Of Note ix

Uncomfortable Truths

Session 1   The Color of Compromise 1

The Colonial Era and the American Revolution

Session 2   Making Race in the Colonial Era 17

Session 3   Understanding Liberty in the Age of Revolution and Revival 31

Slavery and the Civil War

Session 4   Institutionalizing Race in the Antebellum Era 47

Session 5   Defending Slavery at the Onset of the Civil War 61

Jim Crow and Complicity in the North

Session 6   Reconstructing White Supremacy in the Jim Crow Era 75

Session 7   Remembering the Complicity in the North 89

Civil Rights and the Religious Right

Session 8   Compromising with Racism during the Civil Rights Movement 103

Session 9   Organizing the Religious Right at the End of the Twentieth Century . . 119

Racial Reconciliation and the ARC of Racial Justice

Session 10   Reconsidering Racial Reconciliation in the Age of Black Lives Matter . . 133

Session 11   The Fierce Urgency of Now 147

Preface

A WORD FROM JEMAR TISBY

Welcome to *The Color of Compromise Video Study*! This study guide and the twelve video sessions are companion learning experiences to be used with my book *The Color of Compromise: The Truth about the American Church's Complicity in Racism*. The book itself contains the results of my research into the chilling connections between the church and racism throughout American history as well as some of my personal thoughts about how Christians can pursue racial justice. The study explores how Christians have reinforced theories of racial superiority and inferiority and outlines the bold action needed to forge a future of equality and justice. Please note that, due to the nature of the subject, some of the sessions may have graphic content that some viewers may find disturbing.

This study guide and the accompanying video study are designed to help you dig deeper into the topic of racism through personal reflection and biblical engagement, either as an individual or with a group. The study is divided into eleven sessions that correspond to the chapters of the book. In most cases, you will want to read the chapter and watch the corresponding video session prior to working through the content of this study guide. Session twelve is the conclusion to the study and can be watched directly after session eleven.

The sessions can be arranged according to different schedules to fit your specific needs and goals. If you are working through the material as a group or in a class, you may want to cover one session each week over eleven meeting times. Alternatively, some groups may want to combine two sessions into one and work through more material each time they meet. For those who prefer to combine lessons, I recommend the following accelerated meeting schedule:

1. Uncomfortable Truths	Sessions 1
2. The Colonial Era and the American Revolution	Sessions 2 and 3
3. Slavery and the Civil War	Sessions 4 and 5
4. Jim Crow and Complicity in the North	Sessions 6 and 7
5. Civil Rights and the Religious Right	Sessions 8 and 9
6. Racial Reconciliation and the ARC of Racial Justice	Session 10 and 11

If you are doing this video study as an individual you can absorb the material as quickly or as slowly as you would like. What matters is that you engage in the content thoughtfully and intentionally.

My hope is that this study will equip you with a greater understanding of the history of the American church's complicity in and, often, the open promotion of racism. I pray that you will be able to learn from the failures of our forebears and move from a complicit Christianity that compromises with racism to a courageous Christianity that boldly confronts it.

Jemar Tisby

Of Note

The quotations (unless otherwise indicated) interspersed throughout this study guide and the introductory comments are excerpted from the book *The Color of Compromise: The Truth about the American Church's Complicity in Racism* and the video study of the same name by Jemar Tisby. The questions in this study have been written by Tyler Burns in collaboration with Jemar Tisby.

THE COLOR OF COMPROMISE

Racism is one of the most polarizing conversations in our world and in the church. So why should the church wade into this difficult topic? In session 1, we'll make the case for *The Color of Compromise.*

INTRODUCTION

On September 15, 1963, four little girls Addie Mae Collins, Denise McNair, Carole Robertson, and Cynthia Wesley were brutally murdered in a bombing at the Sixteenth Street Baptist Church in Birmingham, Alabama. The vicious attack killed these four girls and injured at least twenty more people. This was one of many such attacks of intimidation and terror that marked a brutal period of the civil rights movement, a time of violent racial tragedy.

In response to this bombing, a lawyer named Charles Morgan Jr. stood in front of a group of his peers and asked this piercing question, "Who did it? Who threw that bomb? . . . The answer should be, 'We all did it.'" Morgan's question echoes today as we begin our study about racism in the history of the American church, and his quote reveals a key truth about what racial *injustice* and the history of racism in America needed to succeed: the compromise of Christianity's biblical and moral convictions. Jemar Tisby points out: "History teaches that there can be no reconciliation without repentance. There can be no repentance without confession. There can be no confession without truth."

The Color of Compromise tells the truth about American church's complicity in racism. The purpose of this study guide is to equip you with the truth so that you can share it with others. Together, we can work toward correcting the American church's embarrassing legacy of complicity regarding systemic racism. This legacy of systemic racism has harmed the lives of ethnic minorities while also sullying the church's witness to the world. That's why it is important to tell the truth.

The truth, no matter how uncomfortable it may be, will set us free from the power of racial injustice. This study guide is designed to challenge everyone who seeks to engage the truth of racial injustice with honesty and hope. Honesty requires us to look back with accuracy. Hope requires us to look forward with anticipation. With honesty and hope, the American church can shift its shameful past of racial injustice into a future of racial healing.

When speaking about racial injustice in the church, it is important to note that we will primarily be speaking about the white church and white Christian responses to Black people in the United States. Not that this is the only divide worth studying. Plenty of other divides can—and should—be explored in depth. And many of the principles covered in this study could be applied more broadly in discussing other forms of racism in the American church.

As you begin this journey, you must be honest and acknowledge how you feel confronting these uncomfortable truths. As Jemar shares with us, this could be a difficult study for several different reasons. Some people who learn these historical facts will characterize the pursuit for racial justice as "Marxist," "liberal," or "divisive." Seeing others respond that way may be frustrating or even painful to hear. Lean in and acknowledge your feelings, remembering that countless other people have faced similar rejection.

Others who watch will be frustrated by the overwhelming task of unlearning the narratives that have been taught to them in the past. These narratives were often taught by people who we trusted to lead us. Identifying and replacing unhelpful teaching with better information will feel painful and, at times, heartbreaking. Do not ignore what you are losing, and honestly grieve what you have lost. No matter when you are taking this journey, remember that it is never too late to do the right thing.

Finally, we encourage you to remember that this study is rooted in Jesus. We believe that the foundation of all reconciliation was accomplished by Jesus on the cross. Peace among racial and ethnic groups is not something we have to achieve by our own wisdom and strength. The foundation has been laid, and we must begin by receiving the work that has been done for us in faith. As we learn the hard truth about racism in the American church, remember to rest in the truth and victory that Jesus provides us.

With this in mind, pay attention to this word from Jemar as we begin: "The American church needs the carpenter from Nazareth to deconstruct the house that racism built and remake it into a house for all nations. My hope for this video series is that you would move from being actively or passively racist to being actively antiracist. I call you to abandon complicit Christianity and move toward a courageous Christianity."

TALK ABOUT IT

True racial reconciliation can never be accomplished without understanding how we have been shaped to understand race and the concept of racial reconciliation. With that in mind, consider the following:

➢ Either describe an experience that has helped shape your understanding of racial reconciliation, or describe a relationship that has helped shape your understanding of race.

_____

_____

_____

_____

_____

_____

_____

_____

_____

_____

_____

_____

_____

_____

KEY TERMS

1. **Racism:** A system of oppression based on race.
2. **Historical survey:** An introduction designed to lead you into further study.
3. **Contingency:** The ability to choose differently.
4. **Complicity:** Silence and passivity instead of confrontation and action.

Not only did white Christians fail to fight for black
equality, they often labored mightily against it.
—*Carolyn DuPont*, Mississippi Praying

VIDEO REFLECTIONS

1 What do you think of the definition that was given for racism (as prejudice plus power)? Have you historically thought of racism as a system or as individual acts? Share a few examples that influenced your belief.

_____

_____

_____

_____

_____

_____

_____

_____

_____

_____

_____

_____

_____

_____

_____

2 Before you began this study, how well would you have said the American church has done in responding to racism and racial injustice? Why?

_____

_____

_____

_____

_____

_____

_____

_____

_____

_____

_____

_____

_____

3 Without acknowledging the discomfort we typically experience when talking about race and racial injustice, we cannot move forward in ways that produce reconciliation and healing. On a scale of one to ten (with ten being unbearable and one being not at all), how uncomfortable does this topic make you feel? Give one or two reasons for your answer.

_____

_____

_____

_____

_____

_____

_____

_____

_____

_____

_____

_____

4 Jemar mentioned two groups of people when he discusses potential reactions to this study. The first group of people adamantly disagrees with the church's complicity in racism. The second group of people are unlearning the narratives of their upbringing. In which group would you place most of your Christian friends? What do you believe has influenced their views on racism?

_____

_____

_____

_____

_____

_____

_____

_____

_____

_____

_____

5 Racism never goes away; it just adapts. Racism has shifted from slavery to Jim Crow to a "racialized" society. What evidence have you seen of this "racialized" society in your circle of influence?

_____

_____

_____

_____

_____

_____

_____

_____

_____

_____

6 The topic of racism is often accompanied by feelings of guilt and shame for many Americans. What feelings do you experience when talking about racism in America?

_____

_____

_____

_____

_____

_____

_____

_____

_____

7 Besides this video series and book, what resources have you studied that have helped shape your perspective on racism in America and in the Christian church?

_____

_____

_____

_____

_____

_____

_____

_____

_____

8   The key idea of this book is that the American church has been complicit in racism, choosing silence over solidarity with the oppressed. How have you seen this complicity at work in your own life?

_____

_____

_____

_____

_____

_____

_____

_____

_____

9   Before you can learn more about what Christians have done in the past, it is important to examine your own life. How many close relationships do you have (in your inner circle of friends) with people of a different ethnicity?

_____

_____

_____

_____

_____

_____

_____

_____

10   As you consider the reputation of the American church, list a few reasons why you believe we are not experiencing racial harmony and justice today.

_____

_____

_____

_____

_____

_____

_____

11 As Christians, we believe Jesus has accomplished reconciliation on the cross through his sacrifice. Why do you believe it is necessary for us to keep this reality at the center of conversations about racism?

_____
_____
_____
_____
_____
_____
_____
_____
_____
_____
_____
_____
_____
_____
_____

12 Talking about racism in the American church can be deeply concerning and can create frustration and strong emotions. What do you hope to achieve with this study?

_____
_____
_____
_____
_____
_____
_____
_____
_____
_____
_____
_____
_____
_____

CLOSING PRAYER

- *Thank God* for the opportunity to learn new information about history and to grow in understanding what can be done in the future.
- *Confess* where you have failed to uphold the dignity of your Black brothers and sisters and where your family may have erred as well.
- *Give* God praise for creating a family of every tribe, tongue, and nation. Acknowledge that more should be done to preserve this diverse family.
- *Pray* for family, friends, and loved ones who are still replaying the narratives of the past.
- *Pray* for peace and flourishing to thrive within the Black community and pray that the American church will promote it.
- *Cry out* to God for the American church to take responsibility in creating and preserving racial healing and justice.

The refusal to act in the midst of injustice is itself an injustice. Indifference perpetuates oppression. . . . Like a boil that can never be cured so long as it is covered up but must be opened with all its ugliness to the natural medicines of air and light, injustice must be exposed, with all the tension its exposure creates, to the light of human conscience and the air of national opinion before it can be cured.

—*Dr. Martin Luther King Jr., "Letter from a Birmingham Jail"*

SESSION 1 PERSONAL STUDY
Between Sessions

PERSONAL REFLECTION

Take time to think and journal about the following question:

➤ How has the conversation about race shaped your life?

_____
_____
_____
_____
_____
_____
_____
_____

➤ What do you think it means that the conversation about race has experienced a resurgence over the past few years? What does this resurgence say about how the American church has failed to address race in the past?

_____
_____
_____
_____
_____
_____
_____

PERSONAL PRAYER JOURNEY

Use a separate journal or the space provided here to write down your prayers:

- Journal your prayers for courage or lament for Black Christians or friends who need to understand their dignity and worth.

_____

_____

_____

_____

_____

_____

_____

_____

_____

_____

_____

_____

_____

_____

_____

_____

- Ask God to show you how you can use your God-given gifts and abilities to affirm the dignity of Black Christians and your Black friends.

_____

_____

_____

_____

_____

_____

_____

_____

_____

_____

_____

_____

_____

_____

DIGGING DEEPER

Understanding the Reputation of the American Church on Race

Consider the passages below. How do they relate to issues of race and racism? Has the American church ignored the teachings of Jesus when it comes to race and the dignity of all people? Use the space provided to collect your thoughts.

Read: Mark 12:30–31

Insight about Jesus's command to love your neighbor as yourself:

_____

_____

_____

_____

_____

_____

_____

How this insight affects my approach to racial justice:

_____

_____

_____

_____

_____

_____

_____

Read: 1 John 4:19–21

Insight about the commandment we have to love others consistently:

_____

_____

_____

_____

_____

_____

How this insight affects my approach to racial justice:

_____
_____
_____
_____
_____
_____
_____
_____
_____
_____

Read: Genesis 1:26

Insight about our human dignity from God:

_____
_____
_____
_____
_____
_____
_____
_____
_____
_____
_____
_____
_____
_____

How this insight affects my approach to racial justice:

_____
_____
_____
_____
_____
_____
_____
_____
_____
_____
_____
_____
_____

Understanding Contingency and Complicity

➤ The principle of contingency tells us that throughout history, individuals and groups made choices, but they could have made different choices. Can you think of one or two examples of contingency through history? And one or two examples from your own life?

-
-
-
-

➤ Many Christians choose silence and passivity instead of confronting systems of racial injustice. Can you think of one or two specific consequences of complicity? Can you name one or two specific consequences of complicity in your life?

-
-
-
-

Pray for opportunities to reverse the consequences of complicity as you promote the dignity of all people and display the love of Jesus to your neighbors.

EXPLORING GREAT RESOURCES

Mississippi Praying by Carolyn DuPont

"Letter from a Birmingham Jail" by Dr. Martin Luther King Jr.

DEEPER LEARNING

If you haven't already, you may want to read chapter 1 of *The Color of Compromise* as you continue reflecting on what God is teaching you through this session. In preparation for your next session, you might want to read chapter 2 of the book.

JOURNAL, REFLECTIONS, AND NOTES

SESSION
2

MAKING RACE IN THE COLONIAL ERA

Understanding racism requires that we head back to its origins in the United States during the colonial period. In this session, we see how race is a construct to justify its existing racism during the colonial era.

INTRODUCTION

History books have often romanticized the colonial era. Many Americans have grown up hearing tales of the colonial expansion, perhaps celebrating some of the events through our holidays. While the colonial era may have been a positive time for those who were colonizing the country, the same cannot be said for Native Americans or African people. The colonial era was not a romantic era for them. It was a time of terror.

Rather than being a force for dignity and equality, the early American church too often compromised and mirrored the racist values of the culture. Even the promise of salvation and church membership came accompanied by the harsh reality that for Black people their souls' freedom would never translate into freedom for their bodies. As the Virginia General Assembly publicly declared in 1667: "It is enacted and declared by this Grand Assembly, and the authority thereof, that the conferring of baptism does not alter the condition of the person as to his bondage or freedom."

While colonial churches drew clear lines around church membership to exclude Black people and accommodate racism, Christians today have an opportunity to make different decisions. We can honor what is good and right. Many Christians in the colonial era chose "dividends over dignity." We must not accept that American racism was inevitable. Every generation has the truth of God's Word and the opportunity to confront the idols of their time and culture.

This period of history reveals the truth that race, religion, and politics have often been tied together in an unholy alliance. Even before the United States was formed into a nation, racism flourished.

Reading about this period of history, the inevitable question that we must ask ourselves is "Why did racism exist in the first place?" Race is not a biblical or biological concept; it is a social construct. The concept of race was created to advance the lie that the color of someone's skin determines their intelligence and worth. It was developed to justify the dehumanizing practice of slavery, as those who sought to benefit economically advanced the narrative that being an ethnic minority or someone of a different skin color removed an individual's intrinsic human worth.

From our study of slavery we learn that the practice of slavery was far worse than many of us first thought. It was an act of terror involving murder and kidnapping as slave traders abducted Black bodies from the continent of Africa, stripped them of worth and dignity, ferried them across the "middle passage" on a perilous journey, and sold them to the highest bidder.

The institution of slavery dehumanized all people, but it was especially difficult for women and children. Many women, even very young women and girls, were subject to repeated sexual assault. Children were abused and discarded when they were no longer of value or considered inconvenient. While this history is difficult to reckon with, we must look honestly at the past if we are to address the problems today and find hope for our future.

> O, ye nominal Christians! Might not an African ask you,
> learned you this from your God, who says unto you, Do unto
> all men as you would men should do unto you?
> —*Olaudah Equiano*

Rather than assigning dignity to ethnic minorities when they arrived on the shores of North America, the American church compromised its biblical convictions by trying to force these individuals and families to leave behind their African culture and accept colonial culture. This colonial culture included a belief that enslaved people were something less than human, property that could be bought and sold. As this unbiblical construction of race flourished in the colonies, the church was largely silent and, worse, at times an active collaborator.

As Jemar told us, "If racism can be made, it can also be unmade." The people who lived in the colonial era made their choices. It's time for us to make our own.

TALK ABOUT IT

It is impossible to work toward racial justice if we cannot acknowledge the depth of the problem that we face. The American church has a race problem. Naming this is key to moving forward together. With this in mind, consider the following:

➢ Reflect on the first time you realized that America has a race problem, or reflect on the first time you realized that the American church has a race problem.

_____

_____

_____

_____

_____

_____

_____

_____

_____

_____

KEY TERMS

1. **The scramble:** The rush of white buyers to claim as many enslaved human beings as possible.
2. **Seasoning:** Training African people in custom, language, and work to prepare them for life as someone enslaved.
3. **Slave code:** Sets of laws that categorized enslaved Africans as property and outlined the rules governing the enslaved and the slaveholder.
4. **Hereditary heathenism:** The belief that, just like a parent can pass down genetic traits to their child, parents can pass down a religion to their child. (This led to the erroneous idea that "Christian" meant European and "heathen" meant Native American or African.)

VIDEO REFLECTIONS

1 Contingency gives us hope that even though things have been done a certain way in the past, they do not have to be this way in the future. What do you hope will change in the way the American church handles the issue of race and racial justice?

_____

_____

_____

_____

_____

_____

_____

_____

2 "Just because race is based on a myth doesn't mean it doesn't have real consequences. It becomes a determining factor in who receives advantages and disadvantages." How has racism shaped the way you view yourself? What advantages or disadvantages do you believe you have because of your skin color?

_____

_____

_____

_____

_____

_____

_____

3 How has racism shaped the way that you view other people and the church?

_____

_____

_____

_____

_____

_____

_____

_____

4   Although race is a social construct, it still has power. What do you believe those in power had to gain by advancing the idea of race?

_____

_____

_____

_____

_____

_____

_____

_____

_____

_____

5   Early explorers referred to Native Americans and Africans as "savages" and "heathens." What are some modern examples of terms or labels used to refer to ethnic minorities or people who are different in some way?

_____

_____

_____

_____

_____

_____

_____

_____

_____

6   This video session describes the horrifying conditions of slavery and refers to something called the "middle passage." What was the most surprising or difficult thing you learned about the condition of enslaved people?

_____

_____

_____

_____

_____

_____

_____

_____

> You declare in the presence of God and before this congregation that
> you do not ask for holy baptism out of any design to free yourself
> from the Duty and Obedience you owe to your master while you live,
> but merely for the good of your soul and to partake of the Grace and
> Blessings promised to the Members of the Church of Jesus Christ.
>
> —*Francis Le Jau's "Baptismal Vows for Slaves"*

7   Olaudah Equiano is quoted as saying, "O, ye nominal Christians! Might not an African ask you, learned you this from your God, who says unto you, Do unto all men as you would men should do unto you?" What do you believe this statement says about the American church and its complicity in slavery at this time? What does it say about the church today?

8   Were you aware that the writer of "Amazing Grace" was the captain of a slave ship? What does this fact tell you about the nature of the relationship between slavery and Christianity?

9 American Christians during the colonial era bought into the concept of "hereditary heathenism," the idea that pathologies of belief or religious views could be passed down through the generational line of Native Americans and Africans. How has this way of thinking influenced modern Christianity?

_____

_____

_____

_____

_____

_____

_____

_____

_____

10 Very few people at this time actually changed their mind or changed their path away from complicity with slavery and racism. What do you believe kept them in that system of dehumanization?

_____

_____

_____

_____

_____

_____

_____

_____

11 The "Baptismal Vows for Slaves" essentially said, "God can have your soul, but we keep your body." In what ways do you see this sentiment continue to play out in our modern world?

_____

_____

_____

_____

_____

_____

_____

_____

_____

12 "If racism can be made, it can also be unmade. We can make different choices."
After listening to the teaching this session and/or reading the chapter, what new
choices are you pledging to make? List a few of them below.

_____

_____

_____

_____

_____

_____

_____

_____

_____

_____

_____

_____

_____

CLOSING PRAYER

- *Thank God* for preserving generations of Black families through the terror of the
  middle passage and the transatlantic journey to enslavement.
- *Confess* where you have accepted or promoted false narratives that continue to
  create false messages of inferiority regarding your Black neighbors.
- *Pray* for those who still believe these narratives and for your Black neighbors
  who are faced with these narratives on a daily basis.
- *Invite* God to convict your heart wherever the vestiges of these false narratives
  still inhabit your mind.
- *Cry out* to God that he would give you discernment as you listen to people talk
  and characterize your Black brothers and sisters.
- *Pray* that the Lord will give you the words of truth to speak in dignifying ways
  that promote the language of reconciliation and flourishing.

I hope it will always be a subject of humiliating reflection to me, that I was,
once, an active instrument in a business at which my heart now shudders.

—*John Newton, "Thoughts on the African Slave Trade"*

SESSION 2 PERSONAL STUDY
Between Sessions

PERSONAL REFLECTION

Take time to think and journal about the following questions:

➤ How has a theology that values souls but not bodies affected your understanding of how Christians should approach issues of racial justice?

_____

_____

_____

_____

_____

_____

_____

➤ Where have you seen the ideas of hereditary heathenism preached and taught in the church? What does this say about how the American church views Black Christians?

_____

_____

_____

_____

_____

_____

_____

PERSONAL PRAYER JOURNEY

Use a separate journal or the space provided here to write down your prayers:

- Ask God to show you how to use your God-given gifts and abilities to bring attention to the problems of racism in our country and in the church.

_____

_____

_____

_____

_____

_____

_____

_____

_____

DIGGING DEEPER

Understanding the Reputation of the American Church on Race

Take time to understand how the American church has ignored the teachings of Jesus when it comes to the dignity of all people. Consider the passages below to help focus your attention on issues of human dignity from a biblical perspective. Use the space provided to collect your thoughts:

Read: Matthew 23:23

Insight about Jesus's criticism of the Pharisees' misplaced attention:

_____

_____

_____

_____

_____

_____

_____

How this insight affects my approach to racial justice:

_____
_____
_____
_____
_____
_____
_____
_____
_____
_____

Read: Galatians 3:28

Insight about the equality that every person should have in Christ:

_____
_____
_____
_____
_____
_____
_____
_____
_____
_____

How this insight affects my approach to racial justice:

_____
_____
_____
_____
_____
_____
_____
_____
_____
_____
_____

Read: James 2:9

Insight about the prohibition of preferential treatment:

_____

_____

_____

_____

_____

_____

_____

_____

_____

_____

How this insight affects my approach to racial justice:

_____

_____

_____

_____

_____

_____

_____

_____

_____

_____

Understanding the Making of Race

➤ The making of race still influences the ways that we view one another and the ways that power is distributed. Can you provide one or two examples of how race has influenced the power dynamics globally? Can you provide one or two local examples?

- •
- •
- •
- •

➢ Many Christians have heard confusing messages about the nature of race and the church. What are one or two messages that you hear from the church on the making of race? Name one or two ways the church's message has influenced your view of the gospel.

-
-
-
-

Pray for opportunities to reverse the consequences of complicity as you promote the dignity of all people and display the love of Jesus to your neighbors.

EXPLORING GREAT RESOURCES

The Baptism of Early Virginia by Rebecca Anne Goetz

The Narrative of the Life of Olaudah Equiano by Olaudah Equiano

DEEPER LEARNING

If you haven't already, you may want to read chapter 2 of *The Color of Compromise* to help you as you continue reflecting on what God is teaching you through this session. In preparation for your next session, you might want to read chapter 3 of the book.

JOURNAL, REFLECTIONS, AND NOTES

UNDERSTANDING LIBERTY IN THE AGE OF REVOLUTION AND REVIVAL

Liberty is a concept that has shaped the United States, but that liberty was only reserved for *some* of its citizens. This session will help you better understand how Black people in particular were excluded from the benefits and blessings of liberty during the American Revolution.

INTRODUCTION

"With liberty and justice for all." History books tell us that the American Revolution was fought over the concept of liberty, and liberty was the motivation for many who came to America and helped found this country. According to our national stories, the founders sought the liberty to choose their own path and the freedom to worship and live as they chose. As good and wonderful as this is, unfortunately that liberty was limited to certain people.

"We hold these truths to be self-evident, that all men are created equal, that they are endowed by their Creator with certain unalienable Rights, that among these are Life, Liberty and the pursuit of Happiness." These famous words from the Declaration of Independence inspired many people with a promise of hope, that the benefits and rights of equality and dignity would be extended to all people. Enslaved people in the colonies knew about the concepts of liberty and attempted to apply them to their own situations. They would soon learn that in many cases these words were nothing but a false hope.

For the Black bodies caught up in the American system of slavery, the notion of liberty for all was a cruel contradiction. "Life, Liberty, and the pursuit of Happiness" only applied to white men. It was not for women, and especially not for people of African descent. Black men, women, and children were stuck in bondage, held captive by liberty's limits. As the fight for liberty led to the Revolutionary War for American independence, enslaved people had to choose who to fight with in the conflict. Some chose to join the Patriot army, while others chose to join the British in anticipation of a promise of freedom. Regardless of their choice, the promise of liberty remained elusive for many.

As enslaved people struggled to obtain liberty for their bodies, they were in pursuit of spiritual freedom as well. Despite the liberating promise of the gospel, the American church remained a place of bondage for enslaved people who became Christians. When they converted and embraced the gospel, enslaved Africans made their professions of faith in segregated services which were designed to convert their souls but not their bodies.

The revivals of the 1700s spread throughout the American colonies and were filled with both promise and contradiction. George Whitefield, the most famous preacher of the time, held massive rallies and preached the gospel to everyone in attendance, whether they were white or Black. Yet he compromised on his biblical convictions when he purchased enslaved human beings to build an orphanage. He compounded his sin, taking it a step further, by convincing the Georgia colony to overturn its prohibition on slavery. Whitefield proclaimed the gospel—yet he still violated its core tenet of love for our neighbors.

Jonathan Edwards Jr. preached against the evil of slavery, even as his father, the acclaimed preacher Jonathan Edwards, had enslaved people of his own. Many church historians fail to mention these evils when they teach about these men and unpack the context of their lives. Christian's today frequently choose to focus on the intellectual contributions these men made to the gospel and the church, not their ethical failures.

Despite the lack of support and even outright opposition from prominent Christian leaders, Black representatives of the gospel worked tirelessly to forge a new path for Black evangelical believers. They took advantage of every opportunity, with some becoming pastors of churches. One notable example was Pastor Lemuel Haynes, who became the first Black person ordained by any Christian fellowship or church in America. His church in Vermont was a pioneering example of the potential for Black contributions to American Christianity. Despite his success, he was eventually run out of his church because of racial bias and prejudice.

Other examples of pioneering Black Christian leaders are Richard Allen and Absalom Jones, who were members of the Methodist Episcopal Church. After sitting in the wrong section of a white church, they were forced to leave before they had even finished saying their prayers. Rather than rejoicing in the fidelity these men showed to the Christian faith, instead the congregations kicked them out of the church. Allen and Jones left the Methodist Episcopal Church altogether and founded the first Black denomination in the United States, the African Methodist Episcopal Church.

While many Americans look back on this period of history as a great example of the fight for a shared promise of liberty, we cannot forget that this liberty had a limited scope. It did not loosen the chains of enslaved Africans or welcome praying Black Christians into equal fellowship in white churches. It did not include the pulpits of Black pastors. This liberty was limited to the those in positions of power.

Racial hierarchy could have been challenged, and perhaps squelched, if the American church had taken a courageous stance against it. Revivalists could have used their considerable influence and ended the practice of slavery entirely. And even if it was not in their power to end it, their opposition would have sent a clear message about where the church should stand on the matter of owning people for profit.

Revolution has its limits. This session has taught us that liberty was denied to those who needed it the most. The good news of the gospel tells us that freedom is given to all who ask for it. Today we must not hoard God's freedom and use it for selfish goals; rather, we should advocate for others and ensure that liberty is within the reach of everyone.

We had not been long upon our knees before I heard considerable scuffling and low talking. I raised my head up and saw one of the trustees. . . . Having hold of the Rev. Absalom Jones, pulling him up off of his knees, and saying, "You must get up—you must not kneel here." Mr. Jones replied, "Wait until prayer is over." Mr. . . . said "No, you must get up now, or I will call for aid and force you away." Mr. Jones said, "Wait until prayer is over, and I will get up and trouble you no more."

—*Richard Allen*

TALK ABOUT IT

We are often taught to believe the best about our country's origins and our national history. Reading *The Color of Compromise* reveals more of the truth about our history and exposes several myths we have been taught. With this in mind, consider the following:

➢ What did you grow up learning about the Revolutionary War? Do you celebrate American holidays commemorating the country? Why or why not?

_____

_____

_____

_____

_____

_____

_____

_____

_____

_____

_____

VIDEO REFLECTIONS

Our country often talks about liberty as something essential to the flourishing of its citizens. What do you believe this liberty should look like for Americans today?

_____

_____

_____

_____

_____

_____

_____

_____

There would be no Black church without racism in the white church.
—*Jemar Tisby*

2 In the Christian faith liberty is a core promise of the gospel and something that deeply matters for our flourishing as followers of Jesus. What do you believe spiritual liberty should look like for followers of Jesus today?

_____

_____

_____

_____

_____

_____

_____

_____

_____

_____

_____

_____

_____

_____

3 Despite the horrors of slavery many enslaved people still turned to Christianity and embraced faith in Jesus. How does it make you feel as you consider their devotion to Christ, even in the midst of their slavery to white men and women who often professed the same faith?

_____

_____

_____

_____

_____

_____

_____

_____

_____

_____

_____

_____

4   Black preachers during this time were forced to preach only to Black audiences, often under white supervision. What are your thoughts about this type of oversight? How would this make you feel if you were limited in this way in preaching the gospel?

_____

_____

_____

_____

_____

_____

_____

_____

5   Some of the most famous preachers of all time have owned enslaved people and advocated for slaveholding. What effect do you think these beliefs may have had on their preaching or understanding of the gospel? What implications might their slaveholding have on the way the gospel is preached today?

_____

_____

_____

_____

_____

_____

_____

6   When faced with the need to build his orphanage, George Whitefield used enslaved people to do the work. What might we learn from this? What does it suggest about the dangers of compromise when presented with an opportunity to profit or even to follow the path of least resistance?

_____

_____

_____

_____

_____

_____

7 Many Christians adopted a theology that separated their faith from social responsibility and justice. What do you believe is the proper role of Christian witness regarding justice and social concerns?

_____

_____

_____

_____

_____

_____

_____

_____

_____

8 "There would be no Black church without racism in the white church." Before hearing this statement, what were some of your perceptions about the Black church in America? How has this statement changed your perception of the Black church?

_____

_____

_____

_____

_____

_____

_____

_____

9 Jonathan Edwards Jr. publicly repudiated the practice of slavery even though his own father owned enslaved people. Where have you seen a similar generational difference, either in your family or in the lives of others you know?

_____

_____

_____

_____

_____

_____

_____

10 In response to mistreatment, Richard Allen and Absalom Jones left their Methodist church to start the African Methodist Episcopal Church, the first Black church denomination. What does this teach us about Black resistance to racism?

_____
_____
_____
_____
_____
_____
_____
_____
_____
_____

11 Revolution was an option for the colonies—as a means to remedy injustice—but not for enslaved people. How has this mindset persisted in our nation since colonial times? Are there opportunities available to most people but not for many Black citizens today?

_____
_____
_____
_____
_____
_____
_____
_____
_____
_____

As a revival movement . . . evangelicalism transformed people within their inherited social setting, but worked only partial and selective transformation on the social settings themselves.
—*Mark Noll*, The Rise of Evangelicalism

12 This session has revealed the inconsistency of the American church and the ways it kept Black Christians from experiencing full liberty. What are some ideas you have to promote liberty and equality among Christians today?

_____

_____

_____

_____

_____

_____

_____

_____

_____

_____

CLOSING PRAYER

- *Thank God* for the spiritual liberty that he offers, praying that you will never take that blessing for granted.
- *Confess* where we have failed to safeguard both the spiritual and social liberty of others.
- *Pray* for those who remain bound in both spirit and body.
- *Cry out* to God in repentance and contrition for the ways the church has been silently complicit in the denial of liberty for others.
- *Lament* all the ways that the church's complicity has placed people in danger.

SESSION 3 PERSONAL STUDY
Between Sessions

PERSONAL REFLECTION

Take time to think and journal about the following questions:

➤ When you think of American liberty, what images come to mind? Describe the people you see in the current vision of American liberty?

_____

_____

_____

_____

_____

_____

_____

_____

➤ How has this view of liberty affected the way people have preached the gospel?

_____

_____

_____

_____

_____

_____

_____

_____

PERSONAL PRAYER JOURNEY

Use a separate journal or the space provided here to write down your prayers:

- Ask God to shape your vision of the future and to create in you a fresh imagination for a future.

_____

_____

_____

_____

_____

_____

_____

_____

_____

_____

- Pray for a vision of liberty that includes people who have been ignored in the past.

_____

_____

_____

_____

_____

_____

_____

_____

_____

_____

_____

DIGGING DEEPER

In this study, we'll take some time to understand how a proper view of the kingdom of God influences our vision of justice and liberty. Consider the passages below and how they can help you grow in your faith. Use the space provided to collect your thoughts:

Read: Amos 5:24

Insight about the importance of justice in the kingdom of God:

_____
_____
_____
_____
_____
_____
_____
_____
_____
_____
_____

How this insight affects my approach to racial justice:

_____
_____
_____
_____
_____
_____
_____
_____
_____
_____
_____

Read: Isaiah 1:17

Insight about doing right by defending others:

_____
_____
_____
_____
_____
_____
_____
_____
_____
_____

How this insight affects my approach to racial justice:

_____
_____
_____
_____
_____
_____
_____
_____
_____
_____

Read: Acts 17:26–27

Insight about how God has created each of us for a specific time:

_____
_____
_____
_____
_____
_____
_____
_____
_____
_____
_____
_____

How this insight affects my approach to racial justice:

_____
_____
_____
_____
_____
_____
_____
_____
_____
_____
_____

Addressing Resistance and Revolution

➤ America was built on the idea of revolution against the status quo. What two examples of revolution stand out to you? How do those examples affect your view of liberty?

- •
- •
- •
- •

➤ America embraced revolution, yet Black resistance was rejected. Can you list one or two examples of Black resistance that have been ignored? And one or two examples of Black resistance in the church?

- •
- •
- •
- •

Pray for opportunities to show the self-sacrificial love of Jesus as you encourage clarity, meaning, and dignity in our post-truth world.

EXPLORING GREAT RESOURCES

The Rise of Evangelicalism by Mark Noll

DEEPER LEARNING

If you haven't already, you may want to read chapter 3 of *The Color of Compromise* to help you as you continue reflecting on what God is teaching you through this session. In preparation for your next session, you might want to read chapter 4 of the book.

JOURNAL, REFLECTIONS, AND NOTES

4

INSTITUTIONALIZING RACE IN THE ANTEBELLUM ERA

The antebellum era is viewed with fondness by many Americans, particularly those in the southern states, who see the period as a symbol of their cultural heritage. This session will show how racism, as well as a national concept of race, became institutionalized during this period of American history and how the American church failed to confront this problem.

INTRODUCTION

The contradictions that characterized the American church's positions on slavery and racism continued during the antebellum era. The ongoing conflict about what real freedom means reached a climax in the bloody and brutal Civil War. For all the intellectual arguments about the morality of slaveholding, one fact remains: thousands of Americans were willing to go to war and die for their right to own human beings.

As Jemar told us in the video, "The racism [of this time] is not remarkable. What was remarkable is that Black people did not abandon the faith altogether." Black Christians refused to allow the evil of slavery and racism to cloud the understanding of the gospel they found in the Scriptures. Following the example of those who came before them, they clung to their faith in God to survive and resist their enslavement.

Before the Civil War was fought, elected officials created a series of compromises that were intended to appease states on both sides of the slavery divide. Both the

North and the South sought compromise, working through slavery in a way that prioritized economic concerns and national unity over the dignity of people made in God's image.

Slavery went far beyond being a heinous practice. In some cases, it was the embodiment of pure evil. Enslaved people were not just chained; they were tortured in every way imaginable: physically, emotionally, psychologically, relationally, and spiritually. The horrors are too great to list here. We must avoid romanticizing this era as nothing more than a mistaken opinion or a wrong choice. Only when we accept American slavery for what it truly was will we be able to correct the mistakes of the past.

Enslaved people were treated as "chattel," or property. They could be used and discarded at will. They had no rights, and enslavers routinely separated families, taking wives from their husbands, children from their parents, and brothers from their sisters. Many of these separations were permanent, never allowing these families the hope of possible reunion. Black men were beaten and abused for the slightest indiscretions to keep them firmly locked "in their place" as enslaved people.

Yet the harshest consequences on the plantation were reserved for Black women. Black women were routinely raped and sexually assaulted and then forced to return to work as if nothing happened. Masters could take their bodies whenever they wanted and reproduce additional slave children without any resistance. While they were pregnant, these women were forced to work at the normal pace—through their entire pregnancy—and after giving birth, they were forced back into the fields to work without any time for recovery. They were abused, raped, beaten, and discarded.

Black women clung to hope amid despair. They had no choice. They were required to work, raise their children, and attend to the master's children as well. Escaping from the plantation meant choosing between personal and familial freedom. A mother carrying children with her meant more chances for capture and death.

Enslaved Black people refused to accept enslavement as their fate. They resisted it in silence—as well as with violence. After hearing of the Haitian Slave Rebellion, several enslaved people in the United States were inspired to break free from their masters. Denmark Vesey and Nat Turner rose up and led violent revolts that changed several things for enslaved people in the South.

Vesey's revolt was halted before it had the opportunity to see the light of day, while Turner's achieved some measure of violent success. At the end of his uprising, fifty-five white men, women, and children were dead. Inevitably, there were consequences for this uprising. Over one hundred Black enslaved people were killed in retaliation, and the rules were changed permanently regarding future gatherings of enslaved people in the South. White oversight was permanently mandated at all church gatherings, including revivals. White pastors and other evangelical Christians at this time refused to speak out against these requirements.

Charles Finney was one example of the compromise of Christian leaders during these divided times. Although he preached a gospel of liberty, advocated for abolition, and even allowed Black people to become members of his church, he would not allow their ordination. He maintained a status quo of exclusion and segregation in the church. Yet what this pivotal moment in American church history required was not compromise but resistance. This era called for an uprising from the American church, yet none came. What might our history as Christian churches in American look like today if we had embraced resistance?

> The being of slavery, its soul and body, lives and moves in the chattel principle, the property principle, the bill of sale principle; the cart-whip, the starvation, and nakedness, are its inevitable consequences.
> —*James W. C. Pennington*

TALK ABOUT IT

The antebellum era revealed the church's compromise with slavery when the moment required resistance. The American church refused to resist the horrors of enslavement and that complicity continues to this day. With this in mind, consider the following:

➢ Name a time when you have seen someone compromise instead of resisting racism or when you should have resisted racism but remained silent.

VIDEO REFLECTIONS

1　This video session began with the story of St. Philip's, the first Black Episcopal parish in New York City. In 1846, the church was refused admission into the annual convention. What theological deficiencies do you think led white Christians to exclude Black Christians who shared their same beliefs and were members in the same denomination?

_____

_____

_____

_____

_____

_____

_____

_____

_____

_____

_____

2　The convention claimed that the exclusion of St. Philip's was not on the grounds of skin color but because of their competence. When have you experienced exclusion? Did this exclusion come from people who were different from you, or did you have a lot in common with them?

_____

_____

_____

_____

_____

_____

_____

_____

_____

3 What did you learn about our country's founding documents like the Declaration of Independence or the Constitution growing up in your history classes? How is that similar or different from what you learned in this session?

_____

_____

_____

_____

_____

_____

_____

_____

4 The key word in many of these agreements is the word *compromise*. Compromise is often seen as a good thing—a means of resolving conflict. But are there times when it is wrong to compromise? What should we understand about the dangerous side of compromise? When might it be wrong to compromise on an issue or principle?

_____

_____

_____

_____

_____

_____

_____

_____

5 Enslaved people were valued based upon their measurable monetary value as property. Do you believe our society still treats people as property in any way today? Why or why not? If so, where have you seen this reality present today?

_____

_____

_____

_____

_____

_____

_____

_____

6   Black women were regularly subjected to rape and sexual assault at the hands of
    their slaveholders. How did these accounts make you feel as you heard them? Even
    though we were not alive then, why might it be important for us to know the evils
    of slavery?

    _____

    _____

    _____

    _____

    _____

    _____

    _____

    _____

7   Harriet Jacobs wrote, "Do not judge the poor desolate slave girl too severely!"
    Historically, Black people have experienced harsh judgment for their actions. When
    have you experienced judgment? How did it make you feel? Why is it wrong when
    others judge us harshly?

    _____

    _____

    _____

    _____

    _____

    _____

    _____

8   The Bible tells us that the two greatest commandments are to love the Lord your
    God with all your heart and with all your soul and with all your mind and to love
    your neighbor as yourself. As you consider today's context of race in America, what
    do you believe it means to love our neighbors? Share a concrete example if you can.

    _____

    _____

    _____

    _____

    _____

    _____

9 This session mentions various revolts in response to slavery. What is the moral argument behind a revolt like this? Are you sympathetic? If you had been an enslaved person at this time, do you think you would have revolted? Why or why not?

_____

_____

_____

_____

_____

_____

_____

_____

_____

10 One of the primary ways white masters exercised control over those they enslaved was by controlling their expression of and understanding of Christianity. Why do you believe enslavers wanted to control the services and worship of Black Christian enslaved people?

_____

_____

_____

_____

_____

_____

_____

_____

_____

11 While some preachers like Charles Finney advocated for abolition, many of those same preachers also supported limiting Black Christian leadership. Do you see similar realities playing out in our modern world? In the church today?

_____

_____

_____

_____

_____

_____

_____

_____

12 What lessons can we learn from the resistance of Black Christians during this time of slavery and segregation? How should we apply these lessons to our lives and our churches?

_____

_____

_____

_____

_____

_____

_____

_____

_____

_____

_____

_____

_____

_____

> But, O, ye happy women, whose purity has been sheltered from childhood, who have been free to choose the objects of your affection, whose homes are protected by law, do not judge the poor desolate slave girl too severely!
> —*Harriet Jacobs,* Incidents in the Life of a Slave Girl

CLOSING PRAYER

- *Thank God* for the opportunity to learn from the resistance of Black Christians during slavery.
- *Confess* the ways that the church has failed to listen to the voices of and follow the examples of Black Christians.
- *Pray* for the courage to love your neighbor as yourself.
- *Invite* the Holy Spirit to reveal the ways you have failed to see the full humanity of your neighbors.
- *Cry out* in lament for the ways the church has exercised unjust control over Black bodies.

SESSION 4 PERSONAL STUDY
Between Sessions

PERSONAL REFLECTION

Take time to think and journal about the following questions:

➢ Enslaved Black people were used for monetary gain and economic exploitation. How have you seen Black bodies taken advantage of today, perhaps for profit or to benefit others?

_____

_____

_____

_____

_____

_____

_____

_____

➢ How does the resistance of Black Christians of the past inspire you to live differently today?

_____

_____

_____

_____

_____

_____

_____

_____

_____

PERSONAL PRAYER JOURNEY

Use a separate journal or the space provided here to write down your prayers:

- Ask God to show you how you can love your neighbors fully.

_____
_____
_____
_____
_____
_____
_____
_____

- Ask God to show you how to advocate for the conditions that will lead them to flourish.

_____
_____
_____
_____
_____
_____
_____
_____
_____

DIGGING DEEPER

Understanding the Glory of God and Humanity

Take time to understand how the glory of God provides clarity to our questions regarding human dignity. Consider the passages below and how they will help you grow in your faith. Use the space provided to collect your thoughts:

Read: Proverbs 31:9

Insight about our responsibility to speak out on behalf of others:

_____
_____
_____
_____
_____
_____
_____
_____
_____
_____

How this insight affects my approach to racial justice:

_____
_____
_____
_____
_____
_____
_____
_____
_____
_____
_____
_____

Read: Colossians 3:11

Insight about how we are all created to be equal in the kingdom of God:

_____
_____
_____
_____
_____
_____
_____
_____
_____
_____

How this insight affects my approach to racial justice:

_____
_____
_____
_____
_____
_____
_____
_____
_____
_____

Read: Micah 6:8

Insight about God's command for us to do justice for others:

_____
_____
_____
_____
_____
_____
_____
_____
_____
_____
_____
_____

How this insight affects my approach to racial justice:

_____
_____
_____
_____
_____
_____
_____
_____
_____

Compromise and Flourishing

➤ God created every person with dignity and designed us all to flourish as image bearers. In which areas do you see the flourishing of Black people being diminished? Can you think of one or two examples within the church?

-
-
-
-

➤ Instead of advocating for dignity, the church compromised with the conditions of the day. How can we correct that compromise in the church today? Which strategies could your church adopt?

-
-
-
-

Pray for the courage to advocate for and promote the dignity of all people and display the love of Jesus to your neighbors.

EXPLORING GREAT RESOURCES

Soul by Soul by Walter Johnson

Incidents in the Life of a Slave Girl by Harriet Jacobs

The Origins of Proslavery Christianity by Charles F. Irons

DEEPER LEARNING

If you haven't already, you may want to read chapter 4 of *The Color of Compromise* to help you as you continue to reflect on what God is teaching you through this session. In preparation for your next session, you might want to read chapter 5 of the book.

JOURNAL, REFLECTIONS, AND NOTES

SESSION
5

DEFENDING SLAVERY AT THE ONSET OF THE CIVIL WAR

Slavery is one of the darkest moments in American history. In this session, we discuss the ways the American church was complicit in defending slavery.

INTRODUCTION

The Civil War was waged on the battlefield . . . and in the church. While men died because of conflicts over the morality of slavery, a fierce argument was also taking place in books, lectures, and pulpits. What does the Bible teach about slavery? As one historian has mentioned, the Civil War was both a national *and* a theological crisis. Ironically, the Bible was at the center of the debate that led our nation into its bloodiest war.

Jemar talked about much of this through the lens of Joshua 5:13, where Joshua asks the commander of the Lord's Army, "Are you for us or for our enemies?" The angel of the Lord responds to his question with an unsettling answer in the following verse: "Neither . . . but as commander of the army of the LORD I have now come." God is on his own side and does not align on human "sides." That's not what those fighting in the armies of the Civil War wanted to hear.

There were ongoing arguments over the right interpretations of the Bible on the matter of slavery. The Civil War was clearly fought over slavery, as the articles of secession for many of the southern states make crystal clear. Men died to defend their ability to own other people as property. And tens of thousands of these soldiers were professing Christians. To make the point clear: Christians sacrificed their lives for the evil practice of owning enslaved people.

The Bible tells us, "'Love the Lord your God with all your heart," and "Love your neighbor as yourself" (Luke 10:27). But for many Americans, enslaved people were not their neighbors. Enslaved people were nothing more than property. Southern Christians and church leaders used the Bible to justify their errant beliefs, and in many cases the government authorities agreed.

The Supreme Court handed down rulings that undermined enslaved people's claims to freedom and liberty. In the famous Dred Scott case, the highest court in the land ruled that Black people were "an inferior order, and altogether unfit to associate with the white race" and that they "had no rights which the white man was bound to respect."

Even President Lincoln, the great emancipator, made it clear that liberation for enslaved Africans was limited at best. In one presidential debate he told the audience, "I am not nor have I ever been in favor of bringing about in any way the social and political equality of the white and black races." Black people continued to be viewed as less than human, both in the courts and in the church.

Those [nonslaveholding] States have assumed the right of
deciding upon the propriety of our domestic institutions;
and have denied the rights of property established in fifteen
of the States and recognized by the Constitution.
—the South Carolina Convention, 1860

As these battles raged, Christian denominations weighed in on the issue of slavery. Methodists split into different sects over their disagreements. The northern faction made it clear that as long as their bishops held enslaved people, they would no longer be in good standing. In disagreement, the southern faction formed their own denomination.

The Baptists followed suit by provoking a conversation about slaveholding missionaries. They were able to press the issue until in 1845 it led to division, and the Southern Baptist Convention was formed to maintain the owning of enslaved human beings. Presbyterians were led by men like R. L. Dabney, who argued for the benefits of slavery, asking: "Was it nothing, that this black race, morally inferior, should be brought into close relations to a nobler race?"

Baptists, Methodists, and Presbyterians went beyond agreement with the status quo on slavery; they altered their denominational structures and theological positions to fit the times. Even today, many members of these denominations are unfamiliar with the history of their denomination or local church.

Confronting the past includes taking a close look at the position our church or denomination took in these moments of conflict. What did our leaders do when faced with the decision to advocate for the dignity and rights of Black people or to compromise and maintain the status quo? What did they say when it was popular to make declarations and statements that were clearly not in line with the gospel? Most importantly, what will we do today? What will we say when we are confronted with racial injustice?

TALK ABOUT IT

This session of the study predominantly talks about the formation of denominations and the ways that racism influenced their formation. Denominations are powerful organizations that shape the perception of the church. With this in mind, consider the following:

➤ What is your denomination's history on race and race relations? Has your church ever made statements about race and race relations? If so, do you know what they have said?

_____

_____

_____

_____

_____

_____

_____

_____

_____

_____

_____

_____

_____

VIDEO REFLECTIONS

1 The Civil War was a national and theological crisis. How does it make you feel hearing that Christians have used the Bible to justify the evils of slavery and the position of the Confederacy?

_____

_____

_____

_____

_____

_____

_____

_____

2 In the video, Jemar quoted Joshua 5:13, where the angel of the Lord says that he is not on anyone's side but his own. How might Joshua 5 aid us in thinking about the theological and ideological divisions we face in talking about race today?

_____

_____

_____

_____

_____

_____

_____

_____

Our position is thoroughly identified with the institution of slavery—the greatest material interest of the world.

—*"A Declaration of the Immediate Causes which Induce and Justify the Secession of the State of Mississippi from the Federal Union," 1861*

3 When you first learned about the Civil War, what were you told was the reason for the conflict? How did that understanding shape your views of the Confederacy?

_____

_____

_____

_____

_____

_____

_____

_____

4 Hundreds of thousands of people died to protect and defend the right to enslave people. Many of them were professing Christians. What might that suggest about our tendency to cling to—and even justify—our sin? Where might we be equally blind today?

_____

_____

_____

_____

_____

_____

_____

_____

_____

5 The Civil War was also a theological and biblical battleground. Many pastors and Christians used the Bible to justify the views of slaveholders and defend slavery as something approved by God. In what ways have you personally heard or seen Christians using the Scriptures to justify racism or other sinful behavior?

_____

_____

_____

_____

_____

_____

_____

6   According to the Dred Scott decision, Black people were considered "an inferior order, and altogether unfit to associate with the white race." Where do you see the ramifications of this idea today? What can we positively promote as truth in response to these wrong ideas and thoughts?

_____

_____

_____

_____

_____

_____

_____

_____

7   President Lincoln is considered by many people to be the great emancipator. Yet even he held some problematic views about Black equality. What does this suggest about human beings holding contradictory ideas? How is it possible for someone to advocate for equality yet not truly believe in it?

_____

_____

_____

_____

_____

_____

_____

_____

8   The Mississippi Articles of Secession state, "Our position is thoroughly identified with the institution of slavery—the greatest material interest in the world." In what ways are Black bodies continually commodified and equated with profit?

_____

_____

_____

_____

_____

_____

> I am not, nor have I ever been, in favor of bringing about in any way
> the social and political equality of the white and black races.
> —*Abraham Lincoln*

9 In the 1800s, a number of Christian denominations split over the issue of slavery. These splits institutionalized racial compromise in the American church. To what extent were you aware of these splits before this study? How does it make you feel to know some of this history?

_____

_____

_____

_____

_____

_____

_____

_____

_____

_____

_____

10 Christians in the 1800s compromised their theological beliefs by twisting the Bible to justify their sinful actions. Why do you think churches and denominations tolerated such erroneous teachings? Should members who disagreed have left or stayed and tried to make change from within?

_____

_____

_____

_____

_____

_____

_____

_____

11 Christians defending the Confederacy believed that God was on their side. They created sophisticated defenses for the institution of slavery. In what way has the Bible been co-opted and used to further political agendas today? Can you name any examples of where you have seen this?

_____

_____

_____

_____

_____

_____

_____

_____

_____

_____

12 What lessons do you believe we can learn from the defenses of slavery Christians gave during this time? What can the church do differently today as we learn about this pivotal period of history?

_____

_____

_____

_____

_____

_____

_____

_____

_____

[Black people are] an inferior order, and altogether
unfit to associate with the white race.

—*Judge Roger Taney*

CLOSING PRAYER

- *Thank God* for the opportunity to partner with God's liberation and justice on earth.
- *Confess* the places where the mentality of churches in the Civil War is still present in churches today.
- *Pray* for the humility to never stop learning about history, strategy, and inequity of race and the church.
- *Invite* God to expose your gaps in knowledge about the past.
- *Cry out* in lament for the ways that the church continues to use the Bible to remain complicit in racial inequity and injustice.

SESSION 5 PERSONAL STUDY
Between Sessions

PERSONAL REFLECTION

Take time to think and journal about the following questions:

➤ How have you seen the Bible used to promote behavior and injustice that is against God's idea of flourishing for all people?

_____

_____

_____

_____

_____

_____

_____

_____

➤ What do you see as the major consequences of people failing to use the Bible appropriately to promote justice and equity?

_____

_____

_____

_____

_____

_____

_____

PERSONAL PRAYER JOURNEY

Use a separate journal or the space provided here to write down your prayers:

- Ask God to create in you the capacity to understand the expansive nature of the Scriptures and how they speak to all of life and the world we live in.

_____

_____

_____

_____

_____

_____

_____

_____

_____

_____

DIGGING DEEPER

Consider the passages below and how they will help you grow in your faith. Use the space provided to collect your thoughts:

Read: Proverbs 28:5

Insight about why those who love the Lord will live justly:

_____

_____

_____

_____

_____

_____

_____

_____

_____

_____

How this insight affects my approach to racial justice:

_____
_____
_____
_____
_____
_____
_____
_____
_____

Read: Psalm 89:14

Insight about God's righteousness and justice:

_____
_____
_____
_____
_____
_____
_____
_____
_____
_____

How this insight affects my approach to racial justice:

_____
_____
_____
_____
_____
_____
_____
_____
_____

Read: Isaiah 61:8

Insight about how God hates evil and wrongdoing:

_____
_____
_____
_____
_____
_____
_____
_____
_____
_____

How this insight affects my approach to racial justice:

_____
_____
_____
_____
_____
_____
_____
_____
_____
_____
_____
_____

➢ The Civil War could have been avoided if churches were willing to take a stand against the misuse of the Bible to defend slavery. Can you think of examples of major events in American history or events in your own life that could have been avoided by holding to what the Bible teaches?

- •
- •
- •
- •

➤ During slavery and the Civil War, Christians witnessed some of the worst acts of dehumanization toward enslaved Africans. Yet many stood by and did nothing to prevent it. Why do you believe these Christians kept silent and remained complicit in the evils of slavery?

-
-
-
-

Pray for the wisdom to use the Bible wisely and accurately for the sake of justice and the dignity of all people as you love your neighbors.

DEEPER LEARNING

If you haven't already, you may want to read chapter 5 of *The Color of Compromise* to help you as you continue reflecting on what God is teaching you through this session. In preparation for your next session, you might want to read chapter 6 of the book.

JOURNAL, REFLECTIONS, AND NOTES

_____
_____
_____
_____
_____
_____
_____
_____
_____
_____
_____
_____
_____
_____

6

RECONSTRUCTING WHITE SUPREMACY IN THE JIM CROW ERA

After the dark period of the Civil War, the philosophy of white supremacy was reconstructed and promoted through a brutal period of racism against Black Americans known as the Jim Crow era. In this session we discuss the brutality and anguish of Jim Crow and how it formed the identity of many Black and white Americans, including those in the Christian church.

INTRODUCTION

The end of slavery was not the end of the conflict over white supremacy in America. As Jemar has repeated many times, "Racism never goes away; it just adapts." After the Civil War, racism adapted into the cruel social reality we now refer to as Jim Crow. Jim Crow, named for a minstrel character in blackface used to mock Black people, was a period of many decades that was just as cruel as the era that came before it. Black Americans were no longer enslaved, but they were far from free.

Whenever Black people find themselves with an apparent opportunity, they are quickly reminded of the ongoing reality of racism. Racists tried to reinterpret the causes of the Civil War by instituting what is known as the "lost cause" narrative. Lost cause mythology had one goal: to reinterpret the story of the lost war by promoting a romantic view of southern society, one built on a supposed unity and mutual understanding between enslaved people and their masters.

According to this narrative, the pre–Civil War South was filled with well-intentioned southern men and women, most of whom were considerate Christians. Yes, they may have owned enslaved people, but for the most part they treated them well, even as part of the family. According to this theory, the South was forced into war by the godless northern armies who invaded them without cause.

Considering what we now know about the history of this country, we know that this is nothing but a lie. Yet many Christians today still hold to some version of this narrative. Despite an extensive history that disproves the lost cause mythology, followers of Jesus are still captive to the concept that the South was good and righteous, the embodiment of a Christian way of life. For those who held to racist beliefs, the lost cause narrative was the perfect alternative history, one that helped them make sense of their Civil War defeat and protect their heritage.

As this mythology spread, it infiltrated Christianity and made it possible to justify domestic terrorism. The Ku Klux Klan, or KKK, is one of the most infamous organizations in American history, known for promoting racial terror and evil throughout the South. The KKK regularly sought to intimidate Black people, keeping them "in their place." While the KKK is often viewed today as an irrational fringe group, the Klan was far more popular and widespread than what we know today.

The Klan worked in tandem with the injustice of Jim Crow laws to create an atmosphere of fear for Black people. Jim Crow laws were written and unwritten rules that determined what Black people could and could not do, often with deadly consequences if the "laws" were broken. Black people were forced to avoid "sundown towns," places where they were not allowed to be seen after the sun had set. These laws vilified interracial relationships and enforced violent consequences if these relationships were discovered.

Of all the consequences of white supremacy, the most brutal and terrorizing was the practice of lynching. Jemar shared the shocking stories of Luther and Mary Herbert, who were killed by an angry white mob. Yet this mob was not just an assortment of angry racists. These were self-professing Christians who performed the lynching on the grounds of a local Black church before an audience of thousands of people.

Recy Taylor was a woman who also experienced the evil of white supremacy when she was kidnapped and raped by a group of white men on the way home from attending church. Taylor passed away in 2017, a reminder of how recent these acts of terror are. They are not a matter of ancient history or the distant past; they affected people who are still alive today. The acts mentioned are a small sample that are representative of thousands of other acts of terror designed to intimidate Black people throughout the South. They were calculated. They were evil. And they were public.

As we consider the horrifying legacy of lynching in the Jim Crow South, we cannot ignore the ways that Christians turned a blind eye to these acts or responded to them with silence. Men, women, and children were brutally murdered, sometimes in the name of Christ. Sadly, many in the Christian church remained silent and complicit in this evil.

TALK ABOUT IT

Our country's racial categories are reinforced by its history of racial terror. Lynching and acts of violence intimidated Black communities and cities for decades and continue to do so today. With this in mind, consider the following:

➤ When was the first time you heard about lynching? Does your city have a history of racial terror? What do you know about it? How might you learn more about it?

_____

_____

_____

_____

_____

_____

_____

_____

_____

KEY TERMS

1. **Sundown town:** A city where after sundown the white people didn't want to see Black people around.
2. **Jim Crow laws:** A set of laws and customs that implemented and enforced racial segregation in the United States.
3. **Lynching:** The extrajudicial murders of Black people, especially during the Jim Crow era; they could be carried out by small posses or large mobs of people, primarily for spectacle and terror.
4. **Freedmen's Bureau (1865):** Formally known as the Bureau of Refugees, Freedmen, and Abandoned Lands, this federal entity was in charge of assisting newly freed Black people in adjusting to life after emancipation.

5. **Lost cause mythology:** A narrative devised to make sense of the Civil War for white southerners; it mythologized the antebellum South as a place of noble virtue, orderly social relations, and Christian character.

VIDEO REFLECTIONS

1 It seems that at every moment of Black progress, the United States regresses and maintains some form of racial hierarchy. Do you agree with that statement? Why or why not? If so, why do you believe this happens?

_____

_____

_____

_____

_____

_____

_____

_____

_____

_____

2 During the reconstruction era, Black Americans made strides in various industries, yet they constantly faced racist resistance from white Christians. Why do you believe white Christians living in the South responded this way after losing the war?

_____

_____

_____

_____

_____

_____

_____

_____

3 The "lost cause" mythology is the romanticizing of the American South during the time of enslavement as a generous time of unity. Have you encountered this narrative before? Where have you seen evidence of it?

_____

_____

_____

_____

_____

_____

_____

_____

_____

4 In attempts to reconcile and unify the North and South, many laws were put in place that limited the social equality of Black Americans. What do you believe the North had to gain from these actions?

_____

_____

_____

_____

_____

_____

_____

_____

_____

_____

5 Jim Crow segregation led to ongoing racial terror for Black Americans in the South. What shocked you most as you learned about the racial terror of Jim Crow laws?

_____

_____

_____

_____

_____

_____

_____

_____

6 The "southern way of life" was used as an excuse to protect the South's reputation after losing the Civil War. How might the romanticized story of this way of life still influence the way Christians think or act today?

_____

_____

_____

_____

_____

_____

_____

_____

7 What do you believe are the long-term consequences of the "lost cause" mythology taking root in Christian hearts and minds?

_____

_____

_____

_____

_____

_____

_____

_____

8 What was your perception of the KKK before watching this video? Did you know they experienced any popularity, or did you imagine that they were merely a fringe organization? How do you think it was possible that an organization like this enjoyed such widespread popularity? What do you think were the costs of opposing the KKK and what it stood for?

_____

_____

_____

_____

_____

_____

_____

_____

9 Lynching is an awful, harrowing practice designed to intimidate the Black community. What do you believe this horrible practice was intended to accomplish? Why do you think it was tolerated by so many people, including many Christians?

_____

_____

_____

_____

_____

_____

_____

_____

_____

_____

10 Jemar mentioned a number of stories of racial terror in this session. Which story affected you the most? Why did this story touch you so deeply?

_____

_____

_____

_____

_____

_____

_____

_____

_____

_____

11 Considering how evil and disturbing this era was, how do you believe that you would have responded to this widespread racial terror if you were alive during this time? Be honest in your assessment.

_____

_____

_____

_____

_____

_____

_____

12 What should the church learn from this era of complicity and compromise? How do you see these or similar patterns at work in our world today?

_____

_____

_____

_____

_____

_____

_____

_____

_____

_____

_____

CLOSING PRAYER

- *Thank God* for the tireless work of scholars and activists who did the difficult work of chronicling the truth and the horrors of racial terror.
- *Confess* the ways that you have ignored the depths of white supremacy in our public and private lives.
- *Pray* for the courage to speak up and take action against acts of racism that create a context of complicity.
- *Invite* God to reveal the ways that white supremacy has infiltrated the church and the world around us.
- *Cry out* in lament for the people who have been damaged and hurt because of the lessons the church has failed to learn from the horrors of white supremacy.

SESSION 6 PERSONAL STUDY
Between Sessions

PERSONAL REFLECTION

Take time to think and journal about the following questions:

➤ How entrenched do you feel white supremacy is in the church today? Give examples of its presence.

_____

_____

_____

_____

_____

_____

_____

➤ When you think about the favoritism show to white expressions, norms, and voices in the American church, what do you believe it will take to reverse the trend and create a more diverse and equitable church?

_____

_____

_____

_____

_____

_____

_____

➤ What do you believe the church can do to educate its members about the horrors of white supremacy in the past and the ways it is affecting the present?

_____

_____

_____

_____

_____

_____

_____

_____

_____

_____

_____

_____

_____

_____

_____

PERSONAL PRAYER JOURNEY

Use a separate journal or the space provided here to write down your prayers:

- Pray on behalf of friends who need to understand the depth of white supremacy. Ask God to show you how you can communicate clearly about human dignity and encourage your friends to confront their complicity.

_____

_____

_____

_____

_____

_____

_____

_____

_____

_____

_____

_____

DIGGING DEEPER

Understanding the Glory of God and Humanity

Consider the passages below and how they will help you grow in your faith. Use the space provided to collect your thoughts.

Read: Proverbs 21:3

Insight about how God prefers righteousness and justice:

_____
_____
_____
_____
_____
_____
_____
_____

How this insight affects my approach to racial justice:

_____
_____
_____
_____
_____
_____
_____
_____

Read: 1 John 3:10

Insight about the true sign of a follower of God:

_____
_____
_____
_____
_____
_____
_____

How this insight affects my approach to racial justice:

_____
_____
_____
_____
_____
_____
_____
_____

Read: Romans 12:9

Insight about how we must resist evil and cling to what is good:

_____
_____
_____
_____
_____
_____
_____
_____
_____
_____

How this insight affects my approach to racial justice:

_____
_____
_____
_____
_____
_____
_____
_____

Supremacy and the Scriptures

➤ White supremacy is built on the belief that one class of people is inherently more valuable and important than other marginalized groups. What are some examples of Jesus's words that refute this idea and give us a better vision of humanity?

- •
- •
- •
- •

➤ White supremacy must be resisted, as it is still present today in many different forms. What do you believe you can do to repent of complicity with white supremacy? What can you begin to do to undermine its power in your life and especially in our churches? List some steps below:

- •
- •
- •
- •

Pray for the boldness to name and to resist white supremacy in every part of life, as you promote the dignity of all people and display the love of Jesus to your neighbors.

DEEPER LEARNING

If you haven't already, you may want to read chapter 6 of *The Color of Compromise* to help you as you continue reflecting on what God is teaching you through this session. In preparation for your next session, you might want to read chapter 7 of the book.

JOURNAL, REFLECTIONS, AND NOTES

REMEMBERING THE COMPLICITY IN THE NORTH

While most people assume racism is a southern problem, this session explores the complicity of the northern parts of the country in racism.

INTRODUCTION

Talking about race in America always leads us to the South. Pictures of slave plantations, the Civil War, and the terror of lynching make the South an easy scapegoat for American racism. Yet Jemar reminded us that "bigotry knows no boundaries." Racism was not just present in the South; it was prevalent in the North as well. And according to some reports, it was sometimes worse.

Christian complicity is not just a southern problem either. Churches across the nation were faced with the choice of how to respond to racism, and many failed the test. Augustus Tolton, a Black man who wished to become a priest in the North, was denied by the Catholic Church in America. Instead, he sought out an education in Rome. After studying in Europe, he returned to the United States to become the first person of known African descent to serve as a priest in America.

The church in the western part of the United States also faced a test of racism with the Azusa Street revival. After receiving a call to ministry, a Black man named William J. Seymour led a revival in the holiness tradition that was characterized by healing, speaking in tongues, and other miracles. Similar to the arrival of the Holy Spirit on the day of Pentecost, the revival began as a symbol of ethnic diversity. One person wrote that at the revival "the color line was washed away in the blood." Yet the racial harmony of the revival soon faded and was rejected by white Pentecostal leaders. Seymour's own mentor said the revival had a "disgusting" similarity to "Southern darkey camp meetings." Even a powerful move of the Holy Spirit could not keep the church from compromising with racism.

> These contenders for the faith constructed their racial notions on the twin pillars of black inferiority and white paternalism.
> —*Mary Beth Swetnam Mathews,* Doctrine and Race

Across the country there was another debate taking place concerning different approaches to the gospel. One group believed in the power of the "social gospel" and the necessity of the Christian faith to address equality and material conditions like poverty and lack of housing and food. Another camp rejected this approach, seeing it as a watering down of the gospel message. This narrow interpretation of the gospel focused on the "fundamentals." While this debate was occurring throughout the American church, Black Christians refused to take a side. The Black church forged its own path forward based on its reading of the Bible and its experience of suffering under the evils of racism in America.

Changes in geography didn't change much for most Black Americans. As they came home from World War I and World War II, Black soldiers were ostracized by a country that accepted their sacrifice abroad but did not support their freedom at home. Both southern and northern soldiers were marginalized by a country that did not value them. Where you lived made little difference. Racism was a national problem, affecting Black Americans in the North and the South, the East and the West, as well as in the American Midwest.

A few decades later, Martin Luther King Jr. experienced this reality firsthand. As an advocate for civil rights throughout the South, he understood better than anyone what racial terror looked like. Yet when King moved his family to the North Lawndale community of Chicago, they were greeted with far deeper racism than they had expected. After arriving, he said, "I have never seen such hate. Not in Mississippi or Alabama. This is a terrible thing."

Unfortunately, human sin is not confined to a specific region. Wherever there are people, there will be racism. As Jemar told us, "The South was the site of some of the most egregious and obvious acts of racism, . . . but Black people faced some of the same forms and at times even more intense forms of discrimination in every part of the nation. Compromised Christianity transcends regions. This is why Christians in every part of America have a moral and spiritual obligation to fight the church's complicity with racism wherever it may occur."

TALK ABOUT IT

This session deals with our false assumptions that racism is solely present in the American South. Even though there are numerous historic examples of racism in all regions of the country, we are still taught that it is primarily a Southern phenomenon. With this in mind, consider the following:

➤ What is your perception of and experience with racism in the South? What is your perception of and experience with racism in the North?

_____

_____

_____

_____

_____

_____

_____

_____

_____

_____

_____

KEY TERMS

1. **Social gospel:** A theological tradition that encouraged Christians to actively engage in politics and reform in their communities
2. **Fundamentalism:** A theological tradition that emphasized the "fundamentals" of the faith and advocated for a separation between Christianity and many issues deemed "political."
3. **Red Summer (1919):** A period of several months of race riots and protests for Black civil rights and against lynching. The protests occurred in dozens of cities across the United States.

VIDEO REFLECTIONS

1 When you think of racism, do you tend to think about it as a "Southern problem"?
    What has this session revealed about the depth of racism across the nation?

_____

_____

_____

_____

_____

_____

_____

_____

_____

_____

2 Jemar mentioned several denominations that have dealt with racism and experi-
    enced racial schisms. How has racism influenced the denomination that raised you?

_____

_____

_____

_____

_____

_____

_____

_____

_____

_____

In many cases, churches not only failed to inhibit white flight
[that is, the exit of white people from cities to suburbs], but actually
became co-conspirators and accomplices in the action.
—*Mark Mulder,* Shades of White Flight

3 The Azusa Street revival shows the limits of spiritual fervor in sustaining racial justice. Where have you seen spiritual clichés and spiritual fervor used as a basis for sustaining racial justice?

_____

_____

_____

_____

_____

_____

_____

_____

_____

4 For fundamentalists, their rally cry regarding the issues of society was akin to "Just preach the gospel." Have you heard this statement before when talking about cultural matters? Do you agree or disagree? What is true about this statement? What is wrong with it?

_____

_____

_____

_____

_____

_____

_____

5 Black Christians in the early 1900s largely avoided the binary choice between the social gospel and the fundamentals. According to Mary Beth Swetnam Mathews, the Black church rejected this "white paternalism." What do you believe the church today can learn from this example? Do we need to choose between preaching the gospel and acting in support of biblical and social justice?

_____

_____

_____

_____

_____

_____

_____

6 Black soldiers who fought for freedom abroad did not receive honor and welcome for their service when they returned home. What would you like to say to such men if you could talk to them today?

_____

_____

_____

_____

_____

_____

_____

_____

7 The "Great Migration" created new tension in northern cities. How have immigration and changing demographics created tension in your city? How should Christians and the church respond?

_____

_____

_____

_____

_____

_____

_____

_____

8 Despite the New Deal being signed into law, Black workers were often left out of its benefits. What do you believe are some of the long-term effects of the New Deal on today's Black families and the loss of generational wealth Black Americans have experienced?

_____

_____

_____

_____

_____

_____

_____

9 Look up the history of the neighborhood you live in right now or the neighborhood you grew up in. For whom was your county, city, or high school named? Is there a Confederate monument in your town? Was there ever a race riot or uprising in your community? How does the history of your neighborhood shape what you think about the place you're living in now?

_____

_____

_____

_____

_____

_____

_____

_____

10 Jemar mentioned that "every region has racism." What is the history of race in your city? How does that racial history affect the way you view your city and its people?

_____

_____

_____

_____

_____

_____

_____

_____

11 How does the perception of covert and overt racism influence the way you confront racism in your life and in your city? How do your beliefs affect the way you see other Christians?

_____

_____

_____

_____

_____

_____

_____

_____

12 This session shows how the effects of racism can permeate every area of our lives. How do you believe that racism has affected the various areas of your personal life, from your day-to-day choices to the big decisions you have made?

_____

_____

_____

_____

_____

_____

_____

_____

_____

_____

_____

_____

CLOSING PRAYER

- *Thank God* for revealing our blind spots and misunderstandings about race and that can we have the opportunity every day to repent, repair, and reconcile.
- *Confess* the ways that you have assumed that only one class of people or region is capable of covert or overt racism.
- *Pray* for eyes to see the racism that is present around you.
- *Invite* God to show you the right steps to take for bringing justice to where you live.
- *Cry out* in lament for the ways we have casually responded to the heinous injustice and mistreatment in our society.

SESSION 7 PERSONAL STUDY
Between Sessions

PERSONAL REFLECTION

Take time to think and journal about the following questions:

➤ Where have you observed white Christians operating in a "paternalistic" mindset toward Black Christians. Give a few examples.

_____

_____

_____

_____

_____

_____

_____

➤ In response to the pursuit of justice many Christians will say "Just preach the gospel." After what you have learned so far in this study, how does this statement fall short of addressing the issues of injustice around us?

_____

_____

_____

_____

_____

_____

_____

PERSONAL PRAYER JOURNEY

Use a separate journal or the space provided here to write down your prayers:

- Pray for the churches in your city to repent of systemic racism. Ask God to show you how you can use your knowledge and wisdom to encourage them toward that repentance.

_____

_____

_____

_____

_____

_____

_____

_____

_____

_____

DIGGING DEEPER

Consider the passages below and how they will help you grow in your faith. Use the space provided to collect your thoughts:

Read: Luke 10:25–37

Insight about protecting others in pain:

_____

_____

_____

_____

_____

_____

_____

_____

_____

How this insight affects my approach to racial justice:

_____
_____
_____
_____
_____
_____
_____
_____
_____
_____

Read: 1 Corinthians 13:1–3

Insight about the importance of loving others:

_____
_____
_____
_____
_____
_____
_____
_____
_____
_____
_____

How this insight affects my approach to racial justice:

_____
_____
_____
_____
_____
_____
_____
_____
_____
_____
_____

Read: 1 John 4:7–8

Insight about loving one another as God does:

_____
_____
_____
_____
_____
_____
_____
_____
_____
_____
_____

How this insight affects my approach to racial justice:

_____
_____
_____
_____
_____
_____
_____
_____
_____
_____
_____

Understanding the Pervasiveness of Racism

➤ Many Christians are resistant to the idea that racism exists in the systems of society and in the way we live. Which resources helped open your eyes to the issues of systemic racial injustice in society?

-
-
-
-

➤ Jesus calls us to pay attention to the needs of people in our communities so that we can promote justice and equity right where we live. List a few areas where your community could improve and become more equitable.

-
-
-
-

Pray for the courage to resist the myth that systemic injustice is confined to one region of the country, especially as you promote human dignity and display the love of Jesus to your neighbors.

DEEPER LEARNING

If you haven't already, you may want to read chapter 7 of *The Color of Compromise* to help you as you continue reflecting on what God is teaching you through this session. In preparation for your next session, you might want to read chapter 8 of the book.

JOURNAL, REFLECTIONS, AND NOTES

_____

_____

_____

_____

_____

_____

_____

_____

_____

_____

_____

_____

_____

_____

_____

_____

_____

SESSION

8

COMPROMISING WITH RACISM DURING THE CIVIL RIGHTS MOVEMENT

The civil rights movement was one of the most important periods in our nation's history in regard to racial justice, yet many churches ignored this opportunity in favor of perpetuating the status quo.

INTRODUCTION

The civil rights movement is the era most people immediately consider when thinking about resistance to racism and racist policies and laws. One of the most significant moments early in the movement involved the tragic killing of young Emmett Till in 1955. Till was only fourteen years old when he was brutally murdered by a gang of white Mississippi men on the suspicion that he had whistled at a white store clerk.

In response to the agony of his murder, his mother, Mamie Mobley Till, resolved to have an open casket so the world could see the horrors of racism for themselves. The story of Emmett Till and others like him were soon burned into the minds of people across the country, especially young Black activists who were resisting racial terror wherever they lived.

Till's memory was clearly on the mind of people like Rosa Parks, who refused to give up her seat for a white passenger on the bus in Birmingham, Alabama. Parks's world-famous moment of civil disobedience lead to the emergence of a larger movement that would promote the civil rights of Black Americans. Parks's refusal to move was followed by a boycott led by a young man named Dr. Martin Luther King Jr.

King is often remembered through a one-dimensional lens, viewed as a figure of hope and reconciliation. Jemar referred to this as the "quotable King." And today King remains a symbol of the pursuit of freedom in the face of evil systemic injustice.

Another pastor was also a household name during this time, but for far different reasons. White evangelist Billy Graham is one of the most famous revivalists of all time, known for his fiery sermons and packed camp meetings. Graham was seen as a Christian leader, perhaps the most famous Christian figure of the century, and he set the standard for the way many white Christians discussed the crucial issue of race in America.

Like most Christians, Graham would never be mistaken for an overt racist who used slurs. He was certainly not a KKK member. But he fell right in line with what King would later call "the white moderate." On the positive side, Graham desegregated his revival camp meetings. But he refused to take a stance in support of King's efforts in the civil rights movement, preferring shorter remarks like "I believe the heart of the problem of race is in loving our neighbor." Yet imagine how significant explicit words of support from him would have been to the cause of racial justice.

In addition to Graham's moderate stances, Christians were further entrenching racism in many of their institutions and schools. Leaders like G. T. Gillespie, the president of Belhaven College, explicitly supported segregation and even argued that the races shouldn't mix on the basis of biology. Christians across the country used similar justifications to justify their inaction against racism.

When responding to the Watts Uprising in 1965 in Los Angeles, King called for the country to consider that "a riot is the language of the unheard." When King said this, Graham preached a message where he called the rioting "a point of anarchy." King used the language of justice. Graham used the language of law and order.

Though the church continued to be complicit in evils of racism, overt racism by Christians was leading people to consider other religions and intellectual systems. The Nation of Islam was a compelling alternative to Christianity because it uplifted and empowered black people while Christians often failed to confront racism within their own ranks. Seeing Christianity's complicity, along with European portraits of Christ as a white man, potential converts began to question the validity of Christianity. Many began to ask, "How can a white Jesus be on the side of Black people?"

Most white Christians followed the compliant, moderate response of Graham over the disruptive justice of King. And the consequences of this choice are tragic to consider. Today, racism remains entrenched in our systems of power, and the church's witness was damaged for generations.

TALK ABOUT IT

The civil rights movement showed the different approaches that Black and white Christians take toward racial justice. Many of us have absorbed a simplistic narrative of the Civil Rights movement. With this in mind, consider the following:

➢ When did you first hear about the civil rights movement? What were you taught that the civil rights movement meant for racism?

_____

_____

_____

_____

_____

_____

_____

_____

_____

I have almost reached the regrettable conclusion that the Negro's great stumbling block in the stride toward freedom is not the White Citizen's Counciler or the Ku Klux Klanner, but the white moderate, who is more devoted to "order" than to justice; who prefers a negative peace which is the absence of tension to a positive peace which is the presence of justice.

—*Martin Luther King Jr., "Letter from a Birmingham Jail"*

KEY TERMS

1. *Brown v. Board of Education* **(1954):** A landmark Supreme Court case that declared segregation in public schools illegal and paved the way or racial desegregation nationwide.
2. **"The Head of Christ" by Warner Sallman:** A painting reproduced over half a billion times depicting Jesus Christ with European features, light skin, auburn hair and blue eyes; it reinforced ideas that Jesus was white.

3. **"Letter from a Birmingham Jail" (1963):** A classic piece of political theology penned by Martin Luther King Jr. In response to white clergy urging moderation and patience in the Civil Rights movement.

VIDEO REFLECTIONS

1 The case of Emmett Till is a deeply disturbing example of racial terror and injustice. Describe how you felt as you listened to his story. Now consider how you would respond if this had happened to a family member or a child of a close friend. How would you feel? What would you do?

_____

_____

_____

_____

_____

_____

_____

_____

_____

2 Martin Luther King Jr. is one of the most influential figures in American history. Yet his memory is often overshadowed by a handful of quotable statements for which he is most widely remembered. Before this study, what was your perception of King? If you had lived during this time, do you believe you would have supported King and his work? Why or why not?

_____

_____

_____

_____

_____

_____

_____

_____

_____

3 Billy Graham is a famous example of how many Christian evangelicals thought and responded to questions of race. What do you believe influenced Graham's refusal to take a resolute stand against racial injustice and inequality? What keeps many evangelicals from doing so today?

_____

_____

_____

_____

_____

_____

_____

_____

_____

_____

4 Did it shock you to hear about Christian appeals to the Bible as the basis for racial segregation? How do you believe these appeals may have influenced modern evangelicalism? Can you think of any examples?

_____

_____

_____

_____

_____

_____

_____

_____

_____

_____

_____

Please help us "Keep Kirkwood White" and preserve our Churches and homes.

—Kirkwood Churches Committee, as cited in Kevin Kruse, White Flight

5 The civil rights movement is often romanticized in our memories, but the truth is that many Christian churches did not stand in solidarity with the protestors. Where do you see the church being equally silent as you consider movements for justice today?

_____
_____
_____
_____
_____
_____
_____

6 "A Call for Unity" was written by a collection of white clergy to Martin Luther King Jr. The letter is filled with reasonable language about timing and tactics and how best to address the problems of racism. In what way do you think similar tactics might be used in today's conversations about racial justice?

_____
_____
_____
_____
_____
_____

7 How did hearing the story about Joseph H. Jackson and the National Baptist Convention change your view of Black church responses during the civil rights movement?

_____
_____
_____
_____
_____
_____

8   The Black power movement is often characterized as a movement of hatred and violence. What did you think about the Black power movement when you first heard of it? How have your thoughts about this movement been changed or altered by this study?

_____

_____

_____

_____

_____

_____

_____

_____

9   Has the principle of "white flight" affected your local community? If you are unaware, take some time to research this phenomenon in your area. What do you think most likely accounts for the reality of white people leaving an area?

_____

_____

_____

_____

_____

_____

_____

_____

10 The most common images of Christ portray him as European instead of the historic reality of Jesus as a Jewish man. How do you believe white European portraits of Jesus have shaped or affected your view of Jesus?

_____

_____

_____

_____

_____

_____

_____

11 The heartbreaking story of Dolphus Weary illuminates the callous nature of white evangelicals in not supporting the civil rights movement. Have you seen any similar stories in your life? In what ways do people mock, make fun of, or otherwise show contempt for racial justice efforts?

_____

_____

_____

_____

_____

_____

_____

_____

_____

_____

_____

12 What lessons have you gleaned from this analysis of the civil rights movement? How will you approach this period of history now that you have studied it from a different angle?

_____

_____

_____

_____

_____

_____

_____

_____

_____

_____

Laughing at Dr. King's death was just like laughing at me or
at the millions of other blacks for whom he labored.
—*Dolphus Weary, 1968*

CLOSING PRAYER

- *Thank God* for the opportunity to learn from the resistance of Black Christians during the civil rights movement.
- *Confess* that for many of us, we too would have been silent on racism during the civil rights movement.
- *Pray* for the courage to stand firm when the modern day issues of race and justice continue to arise.
- *Invite* God to reveal areas where you can take a stand right now.

SESSION 8 PERSONAL STUDY
Between Sessions

PERSONAL REFLECTION

Take time to think and journal about the following questions:

➤ If someone asked you to describe the civil rights movement, what would you say about this time in American history?

_____
_____
_____
_____
_____
_____
_____
_____
_____

➤ What do you believe God thinks about civil disobedience?

_____
_____
_____
_____
_____
_____
_____
_____
_____

➤ How can we take the principles of the civil rights movement and apply them to today? What must be resisted and disobeyed for true justice in our communities?

_____
_____
_____
_____
_____
_____
_____
_____
_____
_____
_____
_____
_____
_____

PERSONAL PRAYER JOURNEY

Use a separate journal or the space provided here to write down your prayers:

• Ask God to give you the boldness to stand firm when you see injustice in your community.

_____
_____
_____
_____
_____
_____
_____
_____
_____
_____
_____
_____

DIGGING DEEPER

Consider the passages below and how they will help you grow in your faith. Use the space provided to collect your thoughts:

Read: Proverbs 18:5

Insight about God's judgment of the guilty:

_____
_____
_____
_____
_____
_____
_____
_____

How this insight affects my approach to racial justice:

_____
_____
_____
_____
_____
_____
_____
_____

Read: Proverbs 17:15

Insight about the consequences for people who justify the wicked:

_____
_____
_____
_____
_____
_____
_____

How this insight affects my approach to racial justice:

_____
_____
_____
_____
_____
_____
_____
_____
_____
_____

Read: Job 34:12

Insight about God always doing what is right:

_____
_____
_____
_____
_____
_____
_____
_____
_____
_____

How this insight affects my approach to racial justice:

_____
_____
_____
_____
_____
_____
_____
_____

Rights and Resistance

➤ When you consider the civil rights movement and the obstacles it faced, what do you believe motivated participants in the face of such danger? List a few things that you believe motivated them.

-
-
-
-

➤ Recently, the issue of white Jesus has become a hotly discussed topic in church and society. When you think of Jesus, what image do you imagine? How do you think that image of Jesus has been shaped by your society?

-
-
-
-

Pray for the courage to resist biased expressions of Christianity as you promote the dignity of all people and display the love of Jesus to your neighbors.

EXPLORING GREAT RESOURCES

White Flight by Kevin Kruse

The Color of Christ by Paul Harvey and Edward J. Bloom

DEEPER LEARNING

If you haven't already, you may want to read chapter 8 of *The Color of Compromise* to help you as you continue reflecting on what God is teaching you through this session. In preparation for your next session, you might want to read chapter 9 of the book.

JOURNAL, REFLECTIONS, AND NOTES

ORGANIZING THE RELIGIOUS RIGHT AT THE END OF THE TWENTIETH CENTURY

In this session, we will be discussing Christian involvement in modern politics. Instead of influencing the political system, the American church has frequently allowed the status quo to influence them into complicit support for racist attitudes and practices.

INTRODUCTION

As we mentioned earlier in our study, race, politics, and religion have always been tied together with the same social bond. The twentieth century provides endless examples indicating that this bond is still present and active. From campaigns to policies to political candidates, religion has been frequently used as a wedge issue in our political discourse. Rather than influencing the political system, Christians have often been carried along by the status quo.

Many Christians supported the idea of color-blind conservatism. Color blindness became a common Christian conservative approach to systemic racism and injustice. You may have heard this idea expressed in various ways. Platitudes like "I don't see color" have often dominated our public discourse, yet this approach effectively silences the grievances of people of color and prohibits progress beyond surface-level changes.

Neither political party in America adequately addresses the problem of racism. During the latter half of the twentieth century the Republican Party branded itself as the party of white evangelical Christians, an identification that continues to the present day. Many evangelical Christians have used this alignment with the Republican Party to create movement and organizations to influence American politics on a national scale.

In the 1970s, Jerry Falwell along with several others created the Moral Majority. This organization was created to be pro-life, pro-family, and pro-liberty. Its goal was to unite Christians as a voting bloc in an effort to shift political discourse in their favor. Yet it also had a sketchy connection to matters of race and racial justice. Rather than using this platform to advocate for racial justice, the Moral Majority advanced racial apathy.

The Moral Majority focused on issues like abortion and private school education as a way to gather support in Christian circles for their initiatives. They drove that support to specific candidates who, in turn, would support their organization and its objections. It was a cycle that benefited both the church and the politician.

The "Religious Right" created written and unwritten rules for Christians to follow in their conversation about politics. Many of the rules revolved around the idea that Christians should be exercising voting power to bend the country toward the right path. The candidates they supported, however, did not often work to create more equitable conditions for people of color. In many cases these candidates actively stood against matters of racial justice.

President Ronald Reagan remains one of the Religious Right's favorite presidents, yet he also aligned himself with problematic racist personalities like Pastor W. A. Criswell and used racially coded language like "welfare queens" during his campaign for president. Reagan famously pushed the War on Drugs, an initiative that put thousands of Black men and women in jail for nonviolent offenses.

Rather than taking a right or wrong approach to political issues, Christians should ask questions to learn why Black and white believers frequently have such divergent political views. Supporting any candidate without critical analysis of an issue and dialogue with opposing views will only create further wedges in the American church. Without honest conversation, the church will continue to remain divided along political lines.

As Jemar told us in this study, "Four hundred years of oppression and white supremacy does not disappear with the stroke of a pen or the passage of just a few years. . . . Christians do have the responsibility to consider how our political allegiances attach themselves in either support for or denial of racial justice. In particular we need to look at the marriage between evangelicalism and conservative politics."

TALK ABOUT IT

As Jemar outlined, the Religious Right and the Moral Majority deeply influenced the way the church approaches politics, especially when it comes to racism. With this in mind, consider the following:

➤ What has the church taught you about politics? Has the presence of racism influenced your politics?

_____

_____

_____

_____

_____

_____

_____

_____

_____

_____

KEY TERMS

1. **Color-blind conservatism:** A style of politics popularized in the 1960s that did not require overtly racist terms in order to enact policies that created and perpetuated racial inequalities
2. **The Religious Right:** a broad coalition of religiously, socially and politically conservative Christians that sought to lobby government officials for the promotion of so-called family values and Christian morality
3. **1976: The year of the evangelical:** A period in which evangelicals, their religion, and especially their political beliefs, captured the attention of journalists and pundits
4. **Bebbington's Quadrilateral:** a widely-used definition of who is an evangelical Christian. It includes four elements: (1) Conversionism, (2) Biblicism, (3) Crucicentrism, and (4) Activism
5. **The southern strategy:** A political tactic that used fears of the Black Civil Rights movement to galvanize an emerging sense of white, middle-class suburban identity and garner votes for the Republican Party
6. **Moral Majority:** A Christian political organization founded by Jerry Falwell who described their values as: pro-life, pro-family, pro-moral, and pro-America

VIDEO REFLECTIONS

1   The video study talks about the idea of "color-blind conservatism." Have you ever believed that we should be "color blind" when it comes to racial reconciliation? What do you find appealing about this idea? What might be problematic about this approach?

_____

_____

_____

_____

_____

_____

_____

_____

2   Race-based language in our country has shifted from explicit slurs to coded language about racial difference. Racism never goes away; it only adapts. How have you seen racism adapting to the changing world around you? List some of the coded racist language (i.e., "dog-whistles) you have heard.

_____

_____

_____

_____

_____

_____

_____

_____

_____

_____

It seems reasonable to assume that when Americans self-identify as evangelicals today, many of them are identifying with the movement as it has taken shape in recent decades—a conservative politicized movement.
—*Hannah Butler and Kristin Du Mez*

3 After hearing the description of evangelicals in the video study, do you consider yourself an evangelical? What is your perception of the term *evangelical* and the ways that it has been used?

_____

_____

_____

_____

_____

_____

_____

_____

_____

_____

4 How has the ideology of the Religious Right affected the world that you live in? Do you see its influence on your Christian friends and in churches?

_____

_____

_____

_____

_____

_____

_____

_____

_____

5 Jemar mentioned that the term *law and order* is a political code phrase used by Richard Nixon to advance a "southern strategy" to get conservative votes. What are other examples of code phrases you have heard that are similar to this? Where do you see these phrases still being used today?

_____

_____

_____

_____

_____

_____

_____

_____

6 What thoughts came to mind when you heard about the origins of the Christian school movement as a continuation of segregated schooling environments? What was your experience with Christian schools? Were they racially diverse? If not, what do you think kept them from racial diversity?

_____
_____
_____
_____
_____
_____
_____
_____

7 According to a sermon by Moral Majority founder Jerry Falwell Sr., "Preachers are not called to be politicians but soul winners." His comments assume that preachers should not be involved in protests or civil disobedience. What do you believe the pastor's role should be in speaking to social issues?

_____
_____
_____
_____
_____
_____
_____
_____

8 What do you believe are the consequences for Christians voting in favor of racist policies?

_____
_____
_____
_____
_____
_____
_____

[Anarchy had been] nurtured by scores of respected Americans including public officials educators clergyman and civil rights leaders as well. . . . I pledge to you we shall have order in the United States.
—*Richard Nixon*

9 It is clear that white and Black Christians vote in completely different patterns. What factors do you believe influence these differences? Have you ever had a conversation with a friend or person of another skin color about their political views and why they support a particular party? If so, what have you learned from that conversation?

_____

_____

_____

_____

_____

_____

_____

_____

_____

_____

_____

10 How do the parallel journeys of Martin Luther King Jr. and Billy Graham reveal something about the ongoing divide between white and Black Christians?

_____

_____

_____

_____

_____

_____

_____

_____

_____

_____

11 According to Jemar, "Christians do have the responsibility to consider how our political allegiances attach themselves to either support or deny racial justice." Which policies do you see as either supporting or denying racial justice?

_____

_____

_____

_____

_____

_____

_____

_____

_____

_____

_____

12 How has this study influenced how you think about your political allegiances and voting practices? Describe a few ways you will think or act differently based upon learning about this evangelical political history?

_____

_____

_____

_____

_____

_____

_____

_____

_____

_____

_____

What galvanized the Christian community was not abortion, school prayer, or the [Equal Rights Amendment]. . . . What changed their minds was Jimmy Carter's intervention against the Christian schools, trying to deny them tax-exempt status on the basis of so-called de facto segregation.

—Paul Weyrich

CLOSING PRAYER

- *Thank God* for the faithful witness of Christians who have resisted the temptation to mold their faith with partisan politics.
- *Confess* the ways that partisan politics has seeped into the church and created unjust policies and politicians.
- *Pray* for the courage to interrogate every area of your life and thinking that has been slanted by the culture wars of the Religious Right.
- *Invite* God to create an openness to think beyond the narrow confines of white evangelicalism.
- *Cry out* in lament for the serious harm that has been done to racial justice and reconciliation in the name of political power.

SESSION 9 PERSONAL STUDY
Between Sessions

PERSONAL REFLECTION

Take time to think and journal about the following questions:

➤ The Religious Right has a strong, deep influence in the minds of many Christians. Where do you see the messages of this stream of thought still being spread?

_____

_____

_____

_____

_____

_____

_____

_____

➤ Many Christians assume that being "color blind" is the right way to approach the issue of race. What do you believe are the relational consequences of this view?

_____

_____

_____

_____

_____

_____

PERSONAL PRAYER JOURNEY

Use a separate journal or the space provided here to write down your prayers:

- Ask God for the wisdom to see where you have believed color-blind theology. Ask God to show you how you can develop a better, more well-rounded view of race and the church.

_____
_____
_____
_____
_____
_____
_____
_____
_____
_____

DIGGING DEEPER

Political Partisanship and the Gospel

Take time to reflect on how partisan politics have influenced the church's approach to human dignity. Consider the passages below and how they will help you grow in your faith. Use the space provided to collect your thoughts:

Read: 2 Thessalonians 1:6

Insight about God's justice:

_____
_____
_____
_____
_____
_____
_____
_____

How this insight affects my approach to racial justice:

_____
_____
_____
_____
_____
_____
_____
_____
_____
_____

Read: Ecclesiastes 3:17

Insight about God's righteous judgment:

_____
_____
_____
_____
_____
_____
_____
_____
_____
_____
_____
_____

How this insight affects my approach to racial justice:

_____
_____
_____
_____
_____
_____
_____
_____
_____
_____
_____
_____

Read: Galatians 6:7

Insight about reaping what we sow:

_____

_____

_____

_____

_____

_____

_____

_____

_____

How this insight affects my approach to racial justice:

_____

_____

_____

_____

_____

_____

_____

_____

_____

_____

_____

_____

Addressing Race and Politics

➤ Imagine that someone asks you to describe your view on politics and faith. How would you answer? List a few of the main descriptions you would use below.

-
-
-
-

➤ What tangible steps can the church take to improve its view of race and guide the political policies that affect shape the lives of Black people and people of color? Can you think of successful strategies that you have seen in this effort?

- •
- •
- •
- •

Pray for the courage to resist biased expressions of Christianity as you promote the dignity of all people and display the love of Jesus to your neighbors.

DEEPER LEARNING

If you haven't already, you may want to read chapter 9 of *The Color of Compromise* to help you as you continue reflecting on what God is teaching you through this session. In preparation for your next session, you might want to read chapter 10 of the book.

JOURNAL, REFLECTIONS, AND NOTES

_____

_____

_____

_____

_____

_____

_____

_____

_____

_____

_____

_____

_____

_____

_____

_____

_____

RECONSIDERING RACIAL RECONCILIATION IN THE AGE OF BLACK LIVES MATTER

In this session, we will discuss the most popular way in which Christians approach race in America: racial reconciliation. Reconsidering racial reconciliation is essential to moving beyond the church's complicity in racism.

INTRODUCTION

When asked what we need to address racism in our country, most Christians would say we need "racial reconciliation." After the civil rights movement, racial reconciliation was the default evangelical approach to addressing the racial divides among us. While *reconciliation* is a word that carries rich biblical meaning, the reality of racial reconciliation has performed well below its lofty expectations.

As a practical strategy, racial reconciliation is frequently accompanied by attempts to create dialogue that places the different sides of the racial divide on equal footing. We commonly hear something like this: "If we can all see the common humanity present in each other, racism will soon fade away."

The latter half of the twentieth century was filled with church movements that offered the promise of diversity and reconciliation between the races. The Southern Baptist Convention repented of its inception in defense of slavery. And the Promise

Keepers movement brought thousands of pastors together to display unity and brotherhood.

With the approach of a new millennium it seemed as if racism was fading away from daily life. Racial slurs and discrimination had become more and more taboo. Yet despite these strategies and real moments of encouragement, racism remained—and still remains.

In the book *Divided By Faith*, Michael Emerson and Christian Smith coined a phrase to describe the time we currently live in: racialized society. Racialized societies create differences in social opportunities and relationships based on a person's skin color and culture. Racism is more than merely the result of a few relationships gone wrong. It is a force embedded into the fabric of our country. Because of this, many are calling for a reconsideration of the effectiveness of racial reconciliation.

A few assumptions empower the belief that racial reconciliation is an effective approach. *Accountable individualism* is the idea that we are all individuals with free will and are accountable for our actions on our own. Yet this idea doesn't allow for the possibility of corporate guilt or the reality of influences outside of a person's agency. *Relationalism* elevates the presence of interpersonal relationships to be preeminent above everything else. In this view, racism is fundamentally caused by misunderstandings or broken relationships. *Antistructuralism* shifts guilt away from systems and structures and advances the idea that structures don't have real power to influence our thoughts and actions.

The white cultural tool kit for addressing race has been thoroughly tested over the last two decades and has often come up short. Consider the beginnings of the Black Lives Matter movement. The creation of the slogan and the subsequent organization were in response to a number of hashtags that commemorated Black men and women who had been killed at the hands of police or white citizens. This slogan created a firestorm in the evangelical church, and names like Michael Brown, Philando Castile, Freddy Gray, Sandra Bland, Eric Garner, and many others received national attention.

Black Lives Matter proved that the work of racial reconciliation did not extend far enough. The cry of lament on behalf of Black image bearers requires that more must be done, beyond the scope of racial reconciliation. The American church must do more than offer displays of diversity and moments of prayer for reconciliation. The church must also stand in solidarity with their neighbors of color.

As Christians of color spoke out in advocacy of this movement to their Christian family, many were ostracized. Leaders like Lecrae, Michelle Higgins, and others received fierce backlash for their public stands. Many of them felt that racial reconciliation did not go far enough, and more was needed. Several cultural factors converged in the 2016 Presidential election when an estimated 80 percent of white evangelicals voted for Donald Trump as president.

> Lament is a liturgical response to the reality of suffering that engages God in the context of pain and suffering.
> —*Soong-Chan Rah*

Christian complicity in racism may look different from previous eras, but it is still present among us today. It includes how we choose to approach racial justice to the silencing of Black Lives Matter to support for a president despite his track record on race. Racism in the American church cannot be overcome by what King called "pious irrelevancies and sanctimonious trivialities." The social, political, and cultural divide requires the church to follow the path of costly *antiracist* action. It requires unprecedented urgency to ensure that the past doesn't become the future.

TALK ABOUT IT

Racial reconciliation has dominated the American church's approach to race recently. Racial reconciliation has also created the conditions for any conversation around race between white and Black Christians. With this in mind, consider the following:

➤ What comes to mind when you hear the term *racial reconciliation*? What, if any, are the flaws of this approach to understanding race and the church?

_____

_____

_____

_____

_____

_____

_____

_____

_____

_____

_____

_____

_____

KEY TERMS

1. **Accountable individualism:** The idea that we are all individuals with free will and are accountable for our actions on our own.
2. **Relationalism:** The belief that social problems are fundamentally due to broken personal relationships rather than systemic or institutional practices.
3. **Antistructuralism:** The idea that structures don't have real power to influence our thoughts and actions.
4. **Racialized society:** A society where in race matters profoundly for differences in experiences, opportunities, and relationships. A society that allocates differential economic political social and even psychological rewards two groups along racial lines that are socially constructed.

VIDEO REFLECTIONS

1 A common evangelical approach to systemic racism has been to promote racial reconciliation. How would you describe racial reconciliation and what does it require? Have you ever been involved in a moment or movement of racial reconciliation? What was the experience like?

_____
_____
_____
_____
_____
_____
_____

2 Where do you see racism in your daily life and in your spheres of influence? What do you feel are the implications for your Black neighbors?

_____
_____
_____
_____
_____
_____

3   In *Divided By Faith*, Michael Emerson and Christian Smith coined the term *racialized society* to describe how racism is still at work in our relationships and society. Give a few examples of how you see our racialized society in your neighborhood and city.

_____

_____

_____

_____

_____

_____

_____

_____

_____

4   The first tool in the evangelical "cultural tool kit" is accountable individualism, the idea that individuals are independent of structures and institutions, have free will, and are accountable solely for their own actions. How is accountable individualism taught in our society?

_____

_____

_____

_____

_____

_____

_____

_____

_____

5   Where have you seen examples of white evangelicals using the cultural tool kit of racial reconciliation to speak about racial justice and race relations? Have you felt it was effective? What are the positives and negatives of this approach, in your opinion?

_____

_____

_____

_____

_____

_____

_____

6   Describe your initial reaction to the phrase "Black Lives Matter." Have your feelings changed at all over time? Why or why not?

_____

_____

_____

_____

_____

_____

_____

_____

_____

_____

_____

7   Which recent instances of police brutality against Black people or people of color stand out to you and why?

_____

_____

_____

_____

_____

_____

_____

_____

_____

_____

8   What does the rise of Black Lives Matter show about the inadequacies of the church's response to racism in America? What is needed from the church at this time?

_____

_____

_____

_____

_____

_____

_____

_____

_____

_____

9 One of the functions of Black Lives Matter is "a cry of lament." What has the role of lament been in your discipleship process? Have the churches you've attended emphasized it? Why might lament be important?

_____

_____

_____

_____

_____

_____

_____

_____

_____

_____

_____

10 Jemar mentioned two people (Lecrae and Michelle Higgins) as examples of people being ostracized for speaking out against the injustice against Black lives. Have you or anyone you know experienced criticism for an opinion on a matter of racial justice as well? Share your or their story.

_____

_____

_____

_____

_____

_____

_____

_____

_____

_____

_____

Lament expresses indignation even outrage about the experience.

—Soong-Chan Rah

11 The 2016 election was a revealing moment in the Christian pursuit of racial justice. How did you observe white and Black Christians reacting to the election results? What do you believe this says about the future of racial justice in the church?

_____

_____

_____

_____

_____

_____

_____

_____

_____

12 What do you believe would help to expand the American church's focus from individual actions to the important issue of systemic solutions?

_____

_____

_____

_____

_____

_____

_____

_____

_____

CLOSING PRAYER

- *Thank God* for the presence of authentic reconciliation that is found in the gospel.
- *Confess* the ways that you have avoided the pursuit of justice because the idea of reconciliation felt easier.
- *Pray* for the Spirit-led imagination to pursue justice in every uncomfortable area that is required to see true change in your life.
- *Invite* the Spirit to show you places where you need to participate in the ministry of reconciliation.
- *Cry out* for God to have mercy on the church for its complicity and compromise in the country's racism.

SESSION 10 PERSONAL STUDY
Between Sessions

PERSONAL REFLECTION

Take time to think and journal about the following questions:

➤ Jemar mentioned a number of police-related shootings of Black men and women from 2012 to 2017. Pick one of these names, write it down, and then do some research to learn more about this person and what happened to him or her. Write down your emotions, feelings, and thought about this incident.

_____

_____

_____

_____

_____

_____

_____

➤ This session talked about the false reconciliation that is often seen in conversations around race. What do you believe healthy reconciliation should look like?

_____

_____

_____

_____

_____

_____

➤ Where have you seen healthy, productive examples of racial reconciliation? What could the church learn from these examples?

_____

_____

_____

_____

_____

_____

_____

_____

➤ What do you believe are the biggest obstacles to racial reconciliation today?

_____

_____

_____

_____

_____

_____

_____

_____

PERSONAL PRAYER JOURNEY

Use a separate journal or the space provided here to write down your prayers:

- Pray for true reconciliation to begin with you and then progress to the church you attend. Ask God to show you how you can use what you are learning in this study to help lead that effort.

_____

_____

_____

_____

_____

_____

_____

DIGGING DEEPER

Take time to reflect on how a better understanding of the gospel provides clarity to our questions regarding racial reconciliation. Consider the passages below and how they will help you grow in your faith. Use the space provided to collect your thoughts:

Read: Job 9:19

Insight about God's character:

_____
_____
_____
_____
_____
_____
_____

How this insight affects my approach to racial justice:

_____
_____
_____
_____
_____
_____
_____

Read: 2 Corinthians 5:11–21

Insight about reconciliation:

_____
_____
_____
_____
_____
_____
_____

How this insight affects my approach to racial justice:

_____

_____

_____

_____

_____

_____

_____

_____

_____

_____

_____

_____

_____

_____

_____

_____

Imagining True Reconciliation

➤ Write out two steps you believe you need to take in order to participate in the effort for true reconciliation. What are two steps that the church should take for true reconciliation to be seen?

-
-
-
-

➤ Reconciliation will not be an easy or simple task. Can you list one or two obstacles that would prevent reconciliation from taking place in the church? And one or two obstacles that would prevent reconciliation in your life?

-
-
-
-

Pray for opportunities to display authentic reconciliation as you promote the dignity of all people and to display the love of Jesus to your neighbors.

DEEPER LEARNING

If you haven't already, you may want to read chapter 10 of *The Color of Compromise* to help you as you continue reflecting on what God is teaching you through this session. In preparation for your next session, you might want to read chapter 11 and the conclusion of the book.

JOURNAL, REFLECTIONS, AND NOTES

_____

_____

_____

_____

_____

_____

_____

_____

_____

_____

_____

_____

_____

_____

_____

_____

_____

_____

_____

_____

_____

_____

_____

_____

THE FIERCE URGENCY OF NOW

What should we do about the racism around us? This session will deal with practical applications that we can practice to partner with the cause of racial justice.

INTRODUCTION

Burdened by the brutality of racism in this country, Dr. Martin Luther King Jr. stepped to the microphone near the Lincoln Memorial in Washington, DC, and delivered his iconic "I Have a Dream" speech. In the address, he tells the crowd that the country desperately needs "the fierce urgency of now." He said, "Now is the time to rise from the dark valley of segregation to the sunlit path of racial justice."

Since King's famous speech, our country has undoubtedly changed. The strides made toward progress in the cause of racial equality and justice cannot overshadow our urgent need for action to address our long national history of racism. We have come a long way, yes, but we still have a long way to go.

Many of you have watched these videos and were deeply moved by the stories or challenged by the information. While those feelings are helpful, it is all too common to feel overwhelmed by the thought of doing something. What is the next step? How can we actually start to change our ways?

In this session we are introduced to a simple pathway to creating a more racially just and equitable society. As Jemar mentioned, these steps are not linear and will not happen overnight, but they provide guidance for us to take the right steps in pursuit of racial justice.

The first thing we must understand is that we do not have the luxury of simply avoiding being racist ourselves. We should all pursue the ideal of treating others with dignity and respect. We should all strive for diverse friendships and connections in our personal and private lives. Yet that alone is not enough. We must intentionally seek to be antiracists, pushing back the evil darkness of systemic racism so that the light of justice and dignity can shine through. This is the only way to avoid complicity with racism.

To this end, Jemar has proposed the ARC of Racial Justice. The ARC consists of three steps that everyone can take to promote racial justice where they live. The first step that the church must embrace is "awareness." While educating ourselves is not enough on its own, nothing truly changes without education. We must become lifelong learners on the history of race in our society and the problems that exist around us. Awareness can take the form of books, documentaries, personal study, classes, or even human sources. Awareness is a lifelong act of refusing to grow complacent in the way things are.

The next aspect of the ARC model is "relationships." Relationships expand our horizons and open up new possibilities for understanding and solidarity. While a book or video will help our minds, relationships have the power to touch our hearts. As Jemar mentioned in this section, "When you know someone, you care about someone. What affects them starts to affect you." We need more people who are willing to be deeply affected by the plight of their neighbors. And that only takes place in the context of deep relationships.

The final aspect of the ARC model for racial justice is "commitment" to action. Once we have learned from history and created relationships with other people, next we must go and do. We cannot simply learn and experience. We must act urgently to create the just society that we desire to see. Action does not have to be national laws or sweeping proposals. Action can be steps of solidarity in neighborhoods, schools, jobs, and churches. Action can be challenging unjust hiring practices or confronting discrimination.

Certainly you will struggle, and at times you will fail to accomplish what you desire. But action is not about perfection. Whatever you do, do something. This is what our study has been about. While we can spend immeasurable time trying to understand the problems, we will not see any progress without a commitment to change what we can.

The church today must practice the good that can be done. To look at our history and then refuse to act only perpetuates racist patterns. It's time for the church to stand against racism and to compromise no longer.

TALK ABOUT IT

Many Christians say that they desire unity within the church, but few have an actual plan in place to achieve that unity. Most churches do not teach concrete steps to achieve that reconciliation. With this in mind, consider the following:

➤ What concrete steps have you been taught that you should take to achieve racial reconciliation? How does the church's strategy for achieving racial justice differ from the culture's strategy?

_____

_____

_____

_____

_____

_____

_____

_____

_____

VIDEO REFLECTIONS

Consider Martin Luther King Jr.'s phrase "the fierce urgency of now." Which areas of society need the most urgent attention in your view?

_____

_____

_____

_____

_____

_____

_____

_____

_____

_____

2 As you've worked through this study, which session made you feel most over-whelmed by the information that was shared? Why?

_____
_____
_____
_____
_____
_____
_____
_____

3 In the ARC of Racial Justice, the first aspect is awareness. How are you planning to increase your racial awareness and education after this study is complete?

_____
_____
_____
_____
_____
_____
_____
_____

4 The second aspect of the ARC of Racial Justice is relationships. As the study mentions, "When you know someone, you care about someone. What affects them starts to affect you." Which relationships have you been most thankful for in your journey toward racial justice?

_____
_____
_____
_____
_____
_____
_____

5 The third aspect of the ARC of Racial Justice is commitment to action. Of the actions that were mentioned in this study, which action resonated most with you? How do you envision yourself getting involved in this cause?

6 Reparations are a controversial topic, yet the video mentions several different layers of reparations from political to ecclesiastical. How do you believe your local church or denomination can get involved with the cause of reparations?

7 In arguing for reparations, Jemar pointed to Daniel 9:8 as a proof of the power of corporate repentance. The verse reads, "We and our kings, our princes and our ancestors are covered with shame, LORD, because we have sinned against you." What is your reaction to the idea of corporate repentance?

8 In thinking about corporate repentance, what is one area that you would repent for on behalf of your family?

_____

_____

_____

_____

_____

_____

_____

_____

_____

9 Does your city have any museums or monuments dedicated to the history of Black people or other people of color? How can you access those museums and symbols and spread the word about them in your community?

_____

_____

_____

_____

_____

_____

_____

_____

10 Jemar said, "If an institution started without an intentional focus on diversity, equity, and inclusion, it's going to be very hard for that institution to add those things in later." What advice regarding race would you give to someone who is considering attending a Christian seminary?

_____

_____

_____

_____

_____

_____

11 What are some practical, actionable steps that you and/or your church can take toward racial justice?

_____

_____

_____

_____

_____

_____

_____

_____

_____

_____

_____

_____

_____

_____

_____

12 James 4:17 says, "If anyone, then, knows the good they ought to do and doesn't do it, it is sin for them." When it comes to racial justice, what do you feel like you should be doing?

_____

_____

_____

_____

_____

_____

_____

_____

_____

_____

_____

_____

_____

_____

CLOSING PRAYER

- *Thank God* for giving you the opportunity to walk through this study and see the church's complicity in racism.
- *Confess* the times you should have acted, and accept the grace of God, which restores us so that we might help restore brokenness elsewhere.
- *Pray for* strength and fortitude for you and your local church community to do everything that you can to promote concretes steps of racial justice.
- *Invite* the Spirit of God to move you toward decisive action in everyday areas of racial justice.
- *Repent* for the ways you and the people you love have been complicit in the furthering of racial injustice.
- *Ask* God for the ability to live out the ARC model for racial justice, for the right awareness/education, the right relationships, and the proper commitment to actionable steps.

SESSION 11 PERSONAL STUDY
Between Sessions

PERSONAL REFLECTION

Take time to think and journal about the following questions:

➤ The church has established pathways for confession, but the route to repairing the spiritual and material harm caused by racism is not as clear. What images come to mind when you hear the word *reparations*? Do you believe it can substantively change the conversation around race in the country?

_____

_____

_____

_____

_____

_____

_____

_____

➤ What other ideas have you seen that you believe can address the church's complicity in racism? How quickly do you believe that these changes can be implemented?

_____

_____

_____

_____

_____

_____

_____

PERSONAL PRAYER JOURNEY

Use a separate journal or the space provided here to write down your prayers:

- Ask God to show you how to bring awareness, relationships, and commitment to action to the conversation about race.

_____
_____
_____
_____
_____
_____
_____
_____
_____
_____

DIGGING DEEPER

Take time to understand how embracing the fierce urgency of now provides motivation for our questions regarding human dignity. Consider the passages below and how they will help you grow in your faith. Use the space provided to collect your thoughts:

Read: Ephesians 2:14

Insight about breaking down the hostility that exists between God and others, as well as between us and others:

_____
_____
_____
_____
_____
_____
_____
_____
_____

How this insight affects my approach to racial justice:

_____
_____
_____
_____
_____
_____
_____
_____
_____

Read: Matthew 5:6

Insight about hungering and thirsting for righteousness in the kingdom of God:

_____
_____
_____
_____
_____
_____
_____
_____
_____
_____

How this insight affects my approach to racial justice:

_____
_____
_____
_____
_____
_____
_____
_____
_____

Embracing the Fierce Urgency of Now

➤ Martin Luther King Jr. emphasized the importance of never forgetting the fierce urgency of now in the pursuit of racial justice. Have you seen examples of urgency from the church? Can you give examples of voices who you hear promoting the same urgency?

-
-
-
-

➤ Jesus tells us that the kingdom of God is at hand. What do you think of when you imagine a diverse kingdom? What characteristics do you believe that kingdom should display?

-
-
-
-

Pray for the motivation and the energy to advance the ARC of Racial Justice in your life and to show the self-sacrificial love of Jesus as you encourage clarity, meaning, and dignity to our post-truth world.

DEEPER LEARNING

If you haven't already, you may want to read the conclusion to *The Color of Compromise.* As we conclude, be sure to watch the final five-minute closing of the video study, session 12.

JOURNAL, REFLECTIONS, AND NOTES